More Best Answers
to the
201 Most
Frequently
Asked
Interview
Questions

Other books by Matthew J. DeLuca and Nanette F. DeLuca

Get a Job in 30 Days or Less: A Realistic Action Plan for Finding the Right Job Fast

Wow! Resumes for Creative Careers

Other books by Matthew J. DeLuca

Best Answers to the 201 Most Frequently Asked Interview Questions

How to Find a Job in 90 Days or Less: A Realistic Action Plan for Finding the Right Job Fast

More Best Answers to the 201 Most Frequently Asked Interview Questions

Matthew J. DeLuca

Nanette F. DeLuca

McGraw-Hill

New York   San Francisco   Washington, D.C.   Auckland   Bogotá
Caracas   Lisbon   London   Madrid   Mexico City   Milan
Montreal   New Delhi   San Juan   Singapore
Sydney   Tokyo   Toronto

McGraw-Hill

A Division of The McGraw·Hill Companies

4   5   6   7   DOC/DOC   0   9   8   7   6   5   4   3

ISBN 0-07-136105-7

The sponsoring editor for this book was Yedida Soloff, the editing supervisor was Maureen B. Walker, and the production supervisor was Charles Annis. It was set in Palatino by Inkwell Publishing Services.

Printed and bound by R. R. Donnelley & Sons.

Contents

Acknowledgments

Many of the questions and situations raised in this book come from real job seekers—just like you. On Job-lnterview.net, we have provided answers to questions posted through the site for the past 2 years. To those job seekers who contacted us, we owe a debt of gratitude for keeping us on our toes and abreast of current interviewing problems. We would like to thank all those who allowed us to help them with their job interview problems.

We also owe a great debt of gratitude to Gary Wong, the vision and force behind Job-Interview.net. It was his idea initially to start the "Q & A" job interview section on the Website, and through his efforts, we will now be appearing on both the Excite Career channel and career.eforce.com.

Betsy Brown is one more person to whom we owe our thanks. She has been instrumental in making our stay with McGraw-Hill a very prolific one. We will really miss her.

Others we want to acknowledge include Cheryl Baldwin, the Assistant Director of the Management Institute at New York University, Linda Stephenson who was born to be a recruiter (and so much more—a real Human Resources pro!) and Maria White—all three colleagues with whom it has been a pleasure to work, and Matt appreciates the confidence each has had in him and the opportunities each has given him to grow professionally in a variety of roles.

Last, a big thank you to Carole Black, President and CEO, and her staff, at Lifetime TV, who retained Matt for nine months of memorable excitement as he worked with all of them to recruit for key positions throughout the organization, in Carole's efforts to bring this leading network to the next level of excellence.

List of Questions

Introduction

Why Do You Need This Book?

Searching for a job is a job in itself! To craft an elegant, targeted résumé and marketing letter is hard work. Networking, searching for job leads and prospects, making telephone call after telephone call, submitting your résumé—they all take an enormous amount of effort. These activities certainly merit the name of job "hunt."

You need time management, organization, and diligence to be successful in your hunt. You have gotten over the procrastination, the shyness, and the frustration. You have set and met goals and priorities. Finally your efforts pay off, and someone at one of the job openings you targeted calls you for an interview! Your résumé may have done the equivalent of "leaping tall buildings in a single bound" to be chosen. Now, you must perform effectively at the interview. **It is not necessarily the best candidate who gets the job offer—it is most likely the best interviewee!**

If it has been more than 3 years since you have last looked for a job, it is a different world from the one you saw when you last ventured forth on a job search. Technology is changing both the workplace and the workers, not to mention the job search process. You can submit your résumé by E-mail, by fax, in person, and by regular mail (now, we have to differentiate between online and "snail mail" services). Your résumé may be reviewed by a software package, not by a person. You can be interviewed over a computer connection or by interactive software. You may be expected to be familiar with all types of technology, from laptops to cell phones.

Did You Know that . . .

❏ The majority of businesses feel that globalization is crucial or at least very important to their business success.

1

❏ One media giant, with headquarters in New York City, filled 25 percent of all job openings in 2000 from postings on the Internet—this compares with less than 5 percent (for almost 1,500 positions) in 1999.

❏ According to the U.S. Department of Labor, there are currently 4 million more job openings in the nation than there are people to fill them.

❏ To bear this out, it is estimated that 20 percent of all software development is delayed because the staff is never found to complete the tasks required.

❏ To add to the shortage, each year only approximately 75 percent of students graduate on time from high school and a vast majority of the remainder never get a high school diploma. Currently there is a huge teacher shortage in the United States; it is estimated that there are 300,000 fewer teachers than the public schools require.

❏ Mass numbers of people are constantly looking for new job opportunities—and they take time away from their employer to do it—surfing the Web for jobs during the workday. To get a leg up, don't do it.

❏ The results of a research study conducted in 1999 showed that the interview can be a predictor of job performance improved to just 32 percent versus 28 percent when the study was completed in 1993. There is a lot of room for improvement in using interviewing in the selection process. Part of the problem stems from the fact that interviewers frequently don't know how to interview. This book will help you to increase the likelihood of success because you the interviewee will become a proficient and effective interviewee and help any employers you get to meet with to become more successful as a result.

The more things change, the more they remain the same:

❏ According to a recent survey conducted by a major outplacement firm, more than 60 percent of all jobs found today are found through networking (versus a 58 percent result in a similar survey done 15 years ago).

❏ People stay in their jobs today an average of 4.2 years (versus 4.1 years in a survey conducted 10 years ago).

❏ Résumés are the introduction to the job search process.

❏ Interviews are the approach of choice.

How Is Work Changing?

Here are just a few examples of how work is changing:

❏ New locations: off-site and telecommuting

❑ New jobs created

❑ New ways of doing old jobs (publishing, marketing, sales, and even grocery shopping)

❑ Increased demand for knowledge workers

❑ New economics: Is E-Commerce required?

❑ New geography: Silicon Valley, Silicon Alley, Silicon Allee`

❑ New costs, new risks, new speeds of doing business

Have you been reading the signs in your field or industry? There is a centipede effect in the workplace. It is no longer a question of waiting for the second shoe to drop (that is, to see the effects of a particular change or event). Now it is more a case of dropping the other shoe . . . and the other shoe . . . and the other shoe . . . . There are multiple ramifications happening faster than ever. A recent example is the mass migration in some areas by lawyers to "dot.com" companies. These start-up enterprises have raised salaries to the point where traditional law firms cannot compete. Some responded in knee-jerk fashion by trying to match the salary levels. This then created a ripple effect and salaries were increased for associates and law clerks. Still, lawyers saw the greener grass and left, causing a shortage of legal talent in many areas. In an attempt to compensate, law firms hired paralegals to fill in the gaps (at much lower salaries) when needed. The firms were then able to pay higher salaries to keep the attorneys on staff by filling vacancies with paralegals. Now, there is a shortage of paralegals, thus causing their salaries to rise accordingly, and law firms are now looking for the next shoe.

The story of the stock market and technology stocks is still being written. Of the "stores" that opened online for the 1999 Christmas selling season, how many were still around for the 2000 (or 2001) holidays? This has caused companies to start and fail, hire and fire employees. The term job security has become an oxymoron. All jobs have become "temporary."

Dealing with the Job Search (and How It Affects Your Interviewing)

You are all fired! Whether you are married or single, have a close family or friends, have been asked to leave your employment or chose to do so yourself, you (and your family and friends) are all out of work. Your job search takes a toll on personal relationships. You take over the kitchen table with your papers. You need a computer all the time (seemingly) for your job search. You don't let anyone use the phone during "working" hours (as you define them). Better yet, don't let anyone else even answer the telephone at all if you are home. When you're out, let the answering machine take it. It sounds more professional. Your job search may have taken over your life, and it has spilled over into your personal relationships.

Have you discussed their role in your search? In addition to bringing you pizza and mailing your letters, are they otherwise involved? Do you want them to be? Have you used them to research leads for you? Do they proofread your résumés and letters? Are they the kind of people who want to hear every nuance of your search or just the bottom line? Do not forget them when you reach the interview stage—use them also for practice interviews and additional research. Then, look forward to a celebration when you land your new job!

What is your commitment? Are you just window-shopping? Are you out of a job right now? Or do you feel that your days are numbered at your current job? Have you been looking unsuccessfully for some time? Do you get asked the same questions and feel that your answers are not quite right? What about your marketing plan—do you feel your approach is dated, not what is being asked for, or slightly dusty for being on the shelf for a seemingly long time? Since the product is you, you may need to make a sale at the interview. Do you feel too old, too fat, too tall, too uneducated, too young, too naive, or too jaded for the job search? Do you have problems with your skills or experience that you cannot correct immediately or do not know how to deal with in an interview? Are you afraid to ask for what you think you are worth?

More Answers Can Answer Your Questions

This book can help you to:

- ❏ Focus and respond
- ❏ Anticipate and investigate
- ❏ Thoroughly prepare
- ❏ Get comprehensive feedback

It is not enough to have gone over a list of questions and answers in preparation for an interview. You need insight into what the interviewer is looking for and why certain questions are asked. You need help in resolving situations before the interview itself. This understanding will help you be prepared, confident, and effective in every interview you participate in.

How to Use This Book

We assume that you are familiar with basic interviewing approaches, such as those covered in our *Best Answers to the 201 Most Frequently Asked Interview Questions* (Best Answers), and you still want additional help. The job market and job searching have changed in the few short years since it was published, and this companion volume will bring you up to date as well as address special problems that you may have.

Whether you have been out of work for over a year, are returning to the job market after an extended period of desired unemployment, have just entered the job market for the first time, or have perceived flaws in your employment or education history, there are ways to deal with each scenario. The issues and situations a new entrant to the workforce must face are not the same as the ones dealt with by someone who was recently fired. Are you considering working for a start-up company? What should you consider first, and what will you be asked? This is not a one-size-fits-all interview guide!

❏ Are you leaving the military, or is your spouse in the military? How do you handle a work history of periodic relocations in an interview?

❏ Never worked? Have recent problems in your personal life made it now necessary for you to look for work, or do you finally have the time to devote to yourself and your career?

❏ If you filed a harassment suit against a prior employer, what do you say in response to the question "Why did you leave that job?"

❏ Have you put your education on hold, or are you changing to part-time student status?

❏ Are you an American citizen returning to the United States after working abroad?

❏ Have you finally completed your studies at night and are ready to make the long-planned career change?

If your answer is yes to any of these questions, then this is the book for you!

The first part of the book, Chapters 1 through 8, will bring you up to date with interview trends and current issues. Specific problems faced in a job interview are covered in Chapters 9 through 13. Guidance in asking the right questions, following up, and negotiating a job offer are discussed in the final chapters, 14 through 17. Look over the Contents as well as the list of questions. Where are your trouble spots?

Your decision to use this book is a sign that you are serious about your job search, and focusing on interviewing skills is the right way to maneuver yourself into your next job. **Suggestion:** Worksheets and exercises are included in this book. Either enlarge and photocopy the forms or use the format in a notebook (a multisubject spiral notebook would be ideal). In either case, do the preparation and research. You will learn about yourself, and you may be surprised!

Which of These Self-Defeating Business Errors Have You Committed?

Playing it too safe. The world is changing more rapidly every day—you need to be a lifelong learner.

Being a know-it-all. Just because that is how "it has always been done" does not mean it still works. Even if you are right, you will be resented for your attitude.

Being unreasonably demanding. Is it "your way or the highway"? You want what you want and you want it now.

Having nothing to fear but . . . Changes are coming whether you are ready or not. Afraid to cut your losses, admit a mistake, and move ahead? Then you may be passed by.

Saying yes! (and yes and yes). Overcommitting will lead to burnout and disappointing others, this ruining your credibility.

Feeling that playing games is beneath you. Politics, small talk, or simply going through the motions are all parts of the business game at one time or another.

Taking it personally. Taking things personally can lead to emotionally charged decisions, such as getting angry and quitting. Quitting too soon eliminates your chances to keep on trying to improve the situation.

Procrastinating. You always seem to wait for the "right" time to make a move; you are late on completing tasks; you're a perfectionist.

Focusing on others. You watch with envy or keep track of their mistakes; this ruins teamwork.

Leaving it up to others. You don't ask for what you need; leaving things to the imagination of others or assuming they know what you need to complete your job.

1

What Is an Interview and Why It Is as Important as Ever

With everything and everyone online, you may feel that face-to-face communications are growing scarce and are less important than they used to be. You can get insurance quotes, buy Avon products (that old door-to-door sales icon) and shop for a medical care provider without leaving your computer. Part-time, freelance, telecommuting, contract, and full-time positions are advertised on the Internet for every conceivable career. Résumés are scanned into databases, video interviews are shown to prospective employers, and interactive application forms are proliferating in the job market. With all these technological advances, there still has been no movement away from the interview as a serious hiring tool. A face-to-face encounter that takes the measure of both interviewee and interviewer is still the method of choice for recruitment and selection. Recent postings in newspapers show that even dot.com companies are hosting job fairs! Although interviews still exist, what may be changing are the abilities of interviewers and interviewees to find the 'right' employee for the 'right' job. As more business is done online, personal communication skills may be suffering.

You still want to meet the person who will repair your car, know about the past performance of a new dentist, and learn about the people you will work with. Verbal and nonverbal communication play an extremely important part in the job search process. All the information you can garner from your research, both online and in the real world, is important, but it is still the interview that will spur a decision. An interview is a two-way opportunity to consider and evaluate all the elements of the organization, the job, and the candidate.

Why Are Interview Questions Good for You?

1. Questions help you understand what the employer needs.

2. Questions help you decide if you want the job.

3. Questions help you communicate in a mutually helpful manner.

What You Need to Know about Interviews

An employment interview is an attempt by the hiring organization to assess three important hiring criteria:

1. **Can do**—the applicant has the education, skills, and training to perform.

2. **Will do**—the applicant has the experience (has performed the same or similar functions in another venue) and possesses the intangible motivation factor.

3. **Fit**—the applicant has experience in a place or environment similar to ours or appears to be able to be easily assimilated into our work team.

These issues are all assessed in a typical 30- to 45-minute interview. At the same time the interviewer also attempts to determine honesty, integrity, enthusiasm, determination, personality, ethics, and potential. The interviewer may be aided by a quick review of the candidate's résumé, augmented by references, testing, work samples, and portfolios. Throughout the meeting, the interviewer should also be taking meticulous notes. This is no mean task for anyone.

Interviewing Is a Skill—on Both Sides of the Desk

You may not have any control over the experience or biases of the interviewer, but you certainly can make yourself into an experienced, competent, confident, and marketable interviewee. You accomplish this by recognizing that both parties, you and the interviewer, are mutually responsible for creating a comfortable, effective interaction.

The failure rate for new hires is high; approximately 40 percent of new executives fail within the first 18 months. Why? Consider these top reasons cited by employers:

1. *"Interpersonal problems. Could not build a working relationship with peers or team."*
2. *"Had no insight into what was expected."*
3. *"Lacked political sense within the organization."*
4. *"Did not meet priorities or main objectives."*
5. *"Longer than expected learning curve."*
6. *"Imbalance between work and personal life."*

How might you prevent such problems?

1. Deal with the current problem, not just the symptoms in hopes it will go away.
2. Push the envelope and "think outside the box." Go outside of your comfort zone in order to make an impact.
3. Be flexible and adapt to different types of people, organizations, and ways of doing things.
4. Keep your cool. Do not allow circumstances to overwhelm you.
5. When there is a tough decision to be made, do the research and make the decision.

Employers and savvy interviewers know these things. They know what the problems are in their organization, and they are extremely interested in making the right hire. These are the issues that drive the questions in the interview!

Shape of an Interview

Think of the last time you had a casual conversation with someone you just met. You may have found some common interests because you were both at the same conference or meeting or on the same airplane. Usually, if you wish to pursue the conversation, you each try to feel each other out for other similarities in your backgrounds or other common denominators. If you find topics that interest you both, then the conversation continues with more sharing and openness. However, should there be any disinclination to share or pursue the conversation on the part of either of you, the conversation winds down and ends.

An interview is as simple as that. The shape of an interview—beginning with small talk—resembles a bell curve with the downside showing the winding down of the process. The height and length of the curve is a measurement of the interest of both parties to continue the process. However, unlike a casual conversation, the interviewer has more control over when to end the conversation, so it is up to you to keep the momentum going if you have an active interest in the job opening or the organization. The sooner the two parties can establish common ground and rapport, the more likely the time will be spent productively exploring the candidate's qualifications and details concerning the job and the organization.

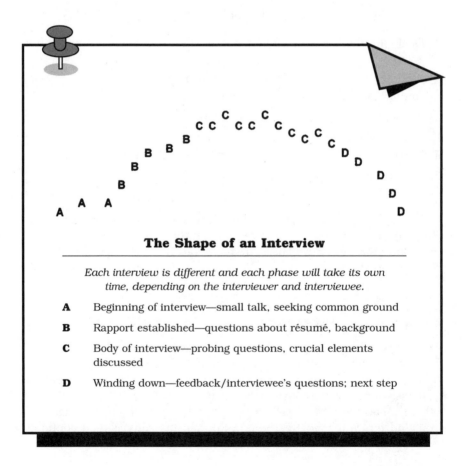

The Shape of an Interview

Each interview is different and each phase will take its own time, depending on the interviewer and interviewee.

A   Beginning of interview—small talk, seeking common ground

B   Rapport established—questions about résumé, background

C   Body of interview—probing questions, crucial elements discussed

D   Winding down—feedback/interviewee's questions; next step

Other Elements of an Interview

Talking versus listening: Casual conversations do not have the high stakes that a job interview has. Throughout your education you have learned to read, speak, and write, but you have spent very little time learning to listen. "Shhhh. Be quiet. Pay attention." When the interviewer speaks, it is important to listen—listen actively rather than think about what you will be saying next. When debriefing yourself after the interview, consider how much time you spent talking versus listening.

Talking about you versus talking about the interviewer: The purpose of the interview is to share information; you want to make your points, and you want to determine whether this is an organization at which you would like to work and a position you wish to pursue. At the same time, the interviewer should be determining whether you are a candidate the organization would want to hire. The important word is *should;* interviewers come in all varieties and abilities. What is being discussed in the interview? The weather for the upcoming weekend? Your skills and accomplishments? The requirements of the job? Depending on the interviewer, you may leave the interview not knowing any more about the job and the organization than you did when you started. On the other hand, an even worse situation can occur—the interviewer can be left knowing little or nothing about you!

Attitude and demeanor: Both you and the interviewer have lives outside the interview; what has happened prior to this meeting can affect either of you positively or negatively. He or she may just not like tall or short people or may have a distrust of people from "big cities." These issues have absolutely nothing to do with your qualifications. A disagreement with a spouse, an important meeting scheduled for later in the day, a bad lunch, or even an uncomfortable pair of shoes can upset the balance of any interview. Misread cues or the tone of your voice may color how the interviewer "reads" you. You are not able to control the interviewer's attitude and demeanor—only your own.

Agendas: Do you and the interviewer have one? Are they the same? First of all, contrary to most popular opinions, most interviewers *want* to like you. They want to be able to hire you (and then go on to the next position or item on his or her work list.) Interviewers want to make it easy on themselves; having you be the perfect candidate would make their lives simpler.

If that were always the case, interviewing would be a lot easier. If hiring the "right" candidate (whatever that is) were the only item on the interviewer's agenda, then the process would be easier. However, not every interviewer has that as the purpose. The organization may already have a candidate in mind and this is just a final "look-see," or the company is just going through the motions to satisfy EEOC (Equal Employment Opportunity Commission) requirements. A worse but sometimes too frequently occurring scenario is that the position is no longer open—an internal transfer has taken place or the position has been eliminated—and the human resources department conducting the interview has not yet been notified.

From the other point of view, the interviewee may just be comparison shopping before accepting another position or trying to up the ante with the current employer by showing that another offer is on the table. Candidates may not be as forthcoming about the circumstances that caused them to leave their last employer or about their responsibilities in prior positions. There may be unexplained gaps in employment that are undisclosed in the résumé. The candidate's professed interest in the organization and the job may be exaggerated; it may be a case of any job right now rather than the right job.

Given all the possible crosscurrents in an interview, stated and hidden agendas, as well as uncontrollable circumstances, an interview is still the prime choice for employers to pick the "right" candidate. And a well-prepared, confident, and knowledgeable candidate can still handle most of the expected and unexpected curveballs thrown during an interview.

Interviewers' Styles

Gather information

Encourage discussion

Create stress

Ask probing questions

Assess behavior

Impose hypothetical situations

Present case interviews

Ask behavioral questions

Format can be:

Structured or unstructured

Or a combination

Types of Interviews

First of all, *interviews can take place anywhere* and can commence at any time. When you are on the telephone, making the appointment or inquiring about job openings, you should consider these actions part of the interview process. You never know whom you may be speaking with or what notes or comments they may make; you have no idea to whom they may pass on their impressions of you or what impression you are making. Additionally, you should also be sizing up the organization by how you are treated on the telephone. Are you placed on hold for an unreasonable length of time; are you disconnected? Does the person you speak with willingly give you his or her name and title? Is there annoying background noise or music? The same goes for your side of the telephone call—is there loud music or a television playing in the background? The environment should be businesslike and courteous on both sides.

When you make an appointment for an interview, you should always know your objective. Why do you want this interview? Is it to gather information or to get leads? Is this person agreeing to see you as a favor to someone else? A *courtesy interview* can be a great way to get inside information about an organization or an industry, but only if the person is knowledgeable and willing to share. Doing research before the interview will assist you in determining what type of help you might expect from this person. *Informational interviews*, used selectively, can target a knowledgeable person who can be asked to share insights into the job market, the industry, or the profession. A question to consider if you want to use the informational interview as part of your job search strategy is whether an informational interview needs to be done in person or are you actually more effective when conducting one over the phone. Our opinion is that the phone approach works effectively because it is less time-consuming and conveys a bias for action that will impress the person you are dealing with. If there is reason to meet, then continue the interview in person (in this situation, the phone call informational interview then may easily become the screening interview).

In response to a job opening or an advertisement, an organization will usually go through a *recruitment and selection process*. The purpose of recruitment is to gather together a pool of candidates from which to choose. Next, the selection process screens—in or out—candidates, leaving the organization with several "top" choices from which to choose the "one." Usually a No. 1 candidate and a backup No. 2 alternate are designated; if No. 1 declines the job offer, the job could be offered to No. 2. Should there not be a sufficient pool of viable candidates recruited, another attempt is made (starting all over by placing ads, listing online, and contacting recruiters) to get more candidates to choose from.

Types of Job Interviews

Face-to-face	Personal interaction
Remote	By telephone, videoconferencing, computer; interviewer is at another site
Group	Several candidates together working on a common task or case study
Panel	Several interviewers meet with the candidate at the same time
Situational	"What if . . ." and hypothetical situations
Behavioral	"Tell me about a time when . . . ."
Case study	Solving problems or resolving situations

Purposes

Recruiting	Attract possible candidates
Screening	Make choices; accept or reject candidates
Selection	Choose the candidate to hire
Hiring	Make the job offer and negotiate employment terms
Due diligence	Cover all the bases
Courtesy	Repay a favor to someone

Screening interviews can be as simple as someone asking whether you have had X number of years experience using a certain machine or technology; or whether you have a college degree. Screening interviews may take place to determine if a candidate should be included or excluded from the first pool of recruits. These can easily be done over the telephone by anyone who is handling the résumés. It shouldn't, but frequently can, be an untrained receptionist or junior clerk. It may also be done by those whose organizations are more serious about attracting people and in those instances screening interviews may include the head of the human resources department, or a recruiter. This basic interview seeks to determine if certain requirements are met, usually in terms of experience, skills, and education. Mass screening interviews are often scheduled by organizations on campus or through job fairs. Sometimes these screening processes eliminate the need for an interview—a cursory review of your résumé will either gather you in or leave you out. (Another reminder of the importance of a targeted, focused résumé and marketing letter.)

Due diligence interviews are conducted when the employer has already identified the "ideal" candidate and is interviewing you to either reinforce that opinion or to meet EEOC requirements. Chances are, you will be given only a cursory session and be told, "Don't call us, we'll call you" as you exit. This can be viewed as a waste of your time or as an opportunity to meet an organization (further openings may arise) and to hone your interviewing skills.

Courtesy interviews occur when a friend of a friend has recommended you. A current employee is a neighbor. Your relatives are members of the same club as the public relations manager. How ever you come in, there may or may not be a suitable job opening. One point in your favor is that most hires are based on referrals. Even if there is not an opening at the moment, this is a terrific opportunity to make a favorable impression, make a powerful contact, and give a great interview!

Moving on to the Next Step

Should you pass the first hurdle, then you will be recruited—invited to come in for a "look-see." Your résumé is reviewed and discussed with you, probably by someone in human resources, and notes are taken. Of prime concern in a *recruitment interview* is usually your past performance; your work history, skills, education and experience. You may ask questions about the organization and about the job opening, but know that the interviewer may have only the knowledge contained in a job requisition form or a job description. He or she may not have a firsthand insight into the position or the department. If you again pass muster, you may be invited back for another interview—the selection interview.

Compared to the recruitment interview, the *selection interview* is typically conducted in more depth and usually by a more senior person at the organization—ideally the manager or someone else from the department or area where you would be assigned if you are offered the job and accept it. There is a truism that line managers, people who are actually doing the work you might be involved with, concern themselves with your potential and are intent upon seeing whether you will fit in with their team and their goals. This is your opportunity to see the work area and your potential supervisor or department head and to get the sense of the organization at work. It is also your opportunity to ask questions that could impact your decision to take the job should it be offered.

You will be participating in a *sequential interview* if you hear something like, *"Do you have the time? There are a few other people I would like to have meet you."* Whether this is sprung on you during a first or second interview spontaneously or you are told in advance that you will be meeting with X, Y, and Z when you come in. These interviews may be with different people in the same division or department that you might be working in or in other, unrelated areas. When you are told you are to see additional interviewers, it is appropriate to ask a few questions in advance:

> *"What is this person's title? Job in the organization? Role in the hiring process?"*

> *"Is this someone I would be expected to work with regularly or sporadically? Report to?"*

> *"How long has she been with the organization? What is his training and experience?"*

Types of Interviewers

Here is a recent story. Recruitment and selection procedures at a tour guide organization included inviting the 100 top candidates for a 2-day outdoor role-playing and behavioral observation session; approximately 35 percent to 50 percent of the candidates present at these events are hired. The organization feels this is the optimal method for evaluating the skills and flexibility that their employees need to think on their feet as tour guides. This is an apt use of a *group interview.*

In an interview situation, you may be faced with more than one individual; a *panel* or *team interview* is one in which you meet with several people from the organization at the same time. The human resources (HR) representative and the department head may decide to meet the candidate together, for example.

Stress interviews, designed to put the candidate in the "hot seat," are passing out of favor. They are still used by some organizations but situational and behavioral interviews are much more in favor. *Situational interviews* are like a one-on-one group interview, in which the candidate is given a hypothetical situation and asked for solutions. In many cases, there is no right answer—it is the candidate's thought processes that are under scrutiny. *Behavioral interviews* are similar, but they concentrate on your past experiences; for example, you are asked to tell "stories" about events and circumstances that have occurred to you and explain your reasoning, actions, and results.

Portrait of an Ideal Interviewer
(from a candidate's point of view)

1. On time and prepared for the interview; has a schedule and plan for the interview.

2. Sets aside time for an uninterrupted interview; informs candidate of approximate length of interview.

3. Has read candidate's résumé and marketing letter.

4. Makes an effort to relax the candidate; makes small talk to establish rapport.

5. Starts with broad statements and questions; then moves into greater detail.

6. Is informed about the job opening; works from a job description or requisition form that outlines the job requirements and responsibilities.

7. Asks open-ended questions to draw out the candidate; takes notes.

8. Does not monopolize the interview; listens more than talks.

9. Is credible; comments are honest; avoids asking illegal questions.

10. Explains clearly to candidate the hiring process and what further steps will be taken by the organization to fill the position.

11. After the interview, fulfills commitments made to telephone or contact candidate with hiring decision.

12. If hired, candidate discovers information provided in interview is accurate.

Another trend in employers' constant search for knowledge workers is the *hypothetical*, *"What would you do . . ."* format. The interviewer poses actual situations that are planned to test your knowledge and experience. A similar format is the *case study approach*, often used to hire consultants, wherein a scenario is described and the candidate's solution or input is sought.

Noninterview Interviews

You never really know when and where you will be interviewed or when you are creating an impression as a possible job candidate. You should have a mini-infomercial about yourself prepared. A two- to three-minute statement that answers the favorite interview question, *"Who are you and why should I hire you?"* This brief, to-the-point sales pitch can be used when you are meeting possible job leads, individuals who may be helpful in your job search, or in response to the dreaded question in an interview.

The telephone is a prime source; many organizations conduct telephone-screening interviews in order to handle the sheer volume of résumés submitted. Those who meet the basic criteria are reached by telephone (by someone junior in HR or the hiring manager) to discuss additional details or questions raised by your résumé. Your voice, telephone manners, and even enthusiasm level can all be construed to your advantage or detriment by the caller.

Career or job fairs provide opportunities for mini-interviews, as do professional gatherings and events. These special events require a modicum of preparation and attention to detail. Written communications—on paper or E-mail—are part of the interview process, in that they either confirm or deny an interviewer's opinion of you and your skills. When you are serious about your job search, even cocktail parties can be occasions for interviews.

Just as some candidates are more experienced than others, there are also interviewers of varying levels of competence. Some may have personalities that conflict with the position, while others may be meeting with you on one of their bad days. You cannot control the circumstance, but you must still be able to present yourself in the best possible light.

If you read business stories, you may see photos of workers with their pets at work. In some of the more casual workplaces, this is the norm. How would you react if, when you entered the office of the interviewer, you were met with a wet nose? That nose would be on the dog, of course. This is another reason for doing preliminary research on an organization before showing up for the interview. Driving by the headquarters and seeing a dog run next to the parking lot might be a clue.

Interviews at holiday time may also present a challenge. A resonant *"Ho ho ho"* and the door opening to reveal Santa Claus interrupted one fellow who was deep into his presentation of his work history. What to do? Why, he took the candy cane offered, wished Santa a happy holiday, too, and then continued with his interview.

Who are you?

Prepare an answer that is no longer than 1 minute covering your professional identity as it relates to the job opening and organization.

Why should we hire you (as opposed to any other equally qualified candidate)?

Prepare an answer that is no longer than 1 minute.

Tell me about yourself.

A concise, targeted and focused 1-minute statement of who you are professionally, related specifically to the interview agenda.

Marketing Yourself

If you have read *Best Answers to the 201 Most Frequently Asked Interview Questions* or any of our other job search books, you know that the first step we advocate taking on the road to a new job is self-assessment. A skills inventory to match what the job/organization needs versus what you have to offer is the focal point of the process. How do you know what the organization needs? By doing research to determine what problems the organization has and then offering yourself as a solution. These "solutions" are your key selling points. This is why your résumé and marketing letters should all be customer-driven and targeted to the specific requirements of each organization and job opening; these documents can be thought of as a "preview of coming attractions," with your interview being the feature presentation.

Marketing itself is undergoing a change, which can affect your job search. Companies are no longer being successful at blasting customers with typical marketing blurbs. Remember all those innovative, humorous dot.com commercials televised at the 1999 Super Bowl? How many of those companies are still in business? Organizations are realizing that they must understand the customer's needs, what is right (or wrong) with their product or services, and get inside the customer's head. Investors are no longer enamored of the dot.com novelty—they are now looking for profits on the bottom line. These trends fit right in with the interviewing tactics we have long advocated: Research is essential to discover what the organization needs and how you can uniquely add value to the organization.

Communication—The Last Frontier in Interviewing

With all the television and radio talk shows, one might think that we are a nation of listeners. We certainly "hear" a lot of talk, but this is not the same as listening. It seems that human nature is against our own best interests; we can hardly stop ourselves from planning our next comment when we hear another person speak. We seemingly cannot miss a beat in promoting ourselves.

How many times have you had either a terrific day or a totally miserable one, with one event triggering another? You run across a friend or you come home to your family looking to regale them with your tale. You get midway into your discourse only to have them say *"Oh, the same thing happened to . . . ."* Now, instead of your talking about what happened to you, you are hearing about what happened to someone else. Others may be so eager to show empathy by illustrating that they know exactly how you feel that you never get a chance to tell them how you feel. They are not listening to you.

This same thing can occur in an interview. The interviewer starts telling an anecdote, and you rush in, interrupting, and start telling a story that shows that you know exactly what he or she was talking about. Or do you? You never gave the interviewer a chance to finish. You were so eager to show your empathy or experience that you did not allow yourself to listen. *Listening is hard.* It forces you to turn your attention to someone other than yourself.

In an interview where your concentration is on *your* skills, *your* need for a job, and *your* need to do well in the interview, turning 100 percent of your attention to someone else's words (and not planning what you will say next while you only half-listen) is a skill that must be practiced. When was the last time someone really listened to you? Did he or she look you in the eye and give you total attention? How did it make you feel? If this has not happened recently, then remember one time when you were frustrated because it was painfully obvious that you were not being listened to? How did you know you did not have the other person's attention?

Active Listening Skills

Maintain eye contact: Break away for thoughtful consideration of questions and responses when necessary.

Repeat the question (use sparingly): Show your understanding and give yourself a moment to form a response. *"If you mean have I had extensive experience with ___ equipment, I used it exclusively for ___ years at ABC Inc."*

Gestures: Hands should be relaxed or used to express excitement. Control any nervous habits.

Tone of voice: Modulate yours to mirror the interviewer's.

Tempo: Speech patterns should complement the interviewer's.

Body language: Lean in to listen, maintaining erect posture. Don't cross your arms over your chest, don't lean on the desk or grip the chair arms. Always be mindful of all other nonverbal messages.

Lose the poker face: Present an honest, open, genuine "pleased to be here" appearance.

2

How to Get Interviews

The search for a job is a building process. It is a puzzle. It is planting seeds. It is searching for a needle in a haystack. It is a dating game. It is a numbers game.

It is all these and more, but regardless of what you consider it, it is a process that requires interviews because without interviews you cannot get a job. Even in a "slam-dunk" situation when you think you have an inside track, you still need to have an interview.

There was a downsizing at a major bank a few years ago. A middle manager who had more than 20 years of service was asked to take early retirement. The bank treated him fairly well by adding additional years of service which improved his retirement benefits and enabled him to continue receiving health benefits into retirement. The bank gave him outplacement assistance, as well. After he left the bank, he took another banking job but with a smaller organization at reduced pay and benefits. He kept in touch with his former boss, with whom he had gotten along so well. After about 8 years, his former boss suggested they have lunch. During the lunch, the employee was offered a similar job to the one he had when downsized. The point is that even though his old boss knew him well, a meeting was still necessary to discuss this matter. If it hadn't gone well, there would have been no job offer. To be offered a job, you always need an interview.

In case you haven't noticed, the topic *"How to get an interview"* is a sneaky substitute for the topic of networking. Networking is a valuable tool and, in fact, is the second best way to get a job. Want to know the best way? It's when people come to you with opportunities before you start to look. In fact, this is an example of networking by someone else. Someone you don't know says to someone who knows you, *"We have an opening to do _____, and it pays _____. Do you know anyone who might be a good candi-*

date?" Then the person who knows you says, *"What about (insert your name)?"* Bingo!

There are two points to be made here. *First*, as good as you may be at interviewing, it is of little use if you do not get a chance to interview because you never get invited to an interview. *Second*, more often than not, one interview will not get you the job, and you need to be successful at each and every interview. You have to get to the next level of interview and the next after that until you have successfully completed all the interview hurdles and been offered the job. So what you need to be is effective at getting more than one interview at each organization that meets with you. Even when you get the offer, the interview process is still not over. You need to get the job offer *and* then successfully complete one more interview at which you need to negotiate items as advantageous to you as possible—without losing the job offer. (See Chapter 16 for two chilling examples of rescinded job offers and other negotiation issues.)

Is it possible to get a job without a résumé? Yes. Is it possible to get a job without an interview? It is very rare. Even the job offer itself takes the interview as a format, whether on the phone or in person. Wise human resources (HR) professionals and managers of every other function like to make the offer personally (and in person if possible) because they relish the idea of performing so positive an act, *and* get confirmation that they are making the right decision.

Now let us make the issue slightly more challenging but also more likely to lead to success. What you need to do is get *relevant* interviews because going through the process of interviewing consumes time and energy. Therefore, if these efforts are not effective, you are putting a lot of energy into a futile activity; that time and effort might be more profitably used elsewhere.

Be Selfish! Know What You Want—Maximize Your Efforts!

The primary reason for an interview is to determine "fit." It is an opportunity for the interviewer to assess whether you, the candidate, are someone the organization should consider offering a job to. Think about it first from the interviewers' perspective. The less they know you, the more they need to determine whether you should be hired—something that is difficult to do because they know so little about you.

Most jobs are never advertised. The reason is that when an opening does occur, it is much easier for an organization to fill the opening with a person it knows (an employee interested in a transfer, a returning former employee (for example, retired or someone who left for a job elsewhere), a relative or friend of a current employee, or a referral from a vendor, client, or supplier. Only when these avenues have been exhausted will the organization look beyond. Even then the organization will not advertise if there is hope that it may find someone through all their contacts.

To get those interviews, what you need to do is become part of this pipeline so that someone in the organization will think of you when an opening occurs and candidates are being sought.

From your standpoint, you need to approach people at an organization—in a selfish manner (What's in this for me?) because they are going to approach you from their selfish perspective (that is, they need to fill this position). From businesses' point of view, it's easier to look at people they know or who come to them from people they know because they will have an experience base and background similarities that will more likely than not be translated into similar behavioral styles (including work ethic). Only failing any referrals from these sources will the employer become more deliberate about making hiring decisions because the employer does not know who it is dealing with. It is not difficult to judge from a résumé whether an applicant has the requisite "hard" (can-do) skills, which may include education and experience. It is more difficult to identify the "soft" (will do and will fit) behaviors, such as how likely is he or she to complete the work in an error-free and in a timely manner, his or her ability to get along with other employees and contacts inside and outside the company, including vendors, suppliers, and customers, how the candidate will handle crises, and how she or he will respond to orders, opportunities, frustrations, and disappointments.

Networking is a process just like interviewing—a means to an end. The essential point to remember is that you don't want to get interviews just to feel good about getting them. You need to make a conscious effort to make the interviews you get meaningful. In order to get interviews that are meaningful, you need to begin the exercise of trying to get interviews with the end—the final result—in mind. Once you get the interview, then you need to meet the objective of the meeting. That too should be clarified as part of your preparation.

The First Interview— How to Get It

It is important to create an image (branding) that presents you as an interesting and creative individual rather than one loaded with gimmicks, who is pushy, and who is boring. When the senior vice president of human resources at the World Wrestling Federation received a metal folding chair with dents, some markings, and a résumé printed on transparent acetate pasted to the seat of the chair, his curiosity was definitely piqued. He figured the job candidate would have some clever follow-up, and he looked forward to the next step. When the candidate, a recent college graduate, called, the vice president took the call because from all the résumés he had received, he let the fellow know he remembered his name from the chair. He asked him why he went through the costly exercise of sending the chair; the candidate answered, *"Hey, you do what you have to do."* The executive was disappointed at the weak response and realized that the chair was merely a gimmick (like résumés on a hockey puck or a soccer ball). Needless to say the candidate never got an interview.

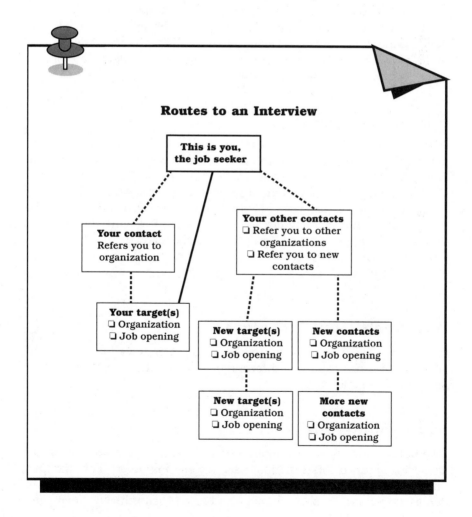

Routes to an Interview

This is you, the job seeker

Your contact
Refers you to organization

Your other contacts
❏ Refer you to other organizations
❏ Refer you to new contacts

Your target(s)
❏ Organization
❏ Job opening

New target(s)
❏ Organization
❏ Job opening

New contacts
❏ Organization
❏ Job opening

New target(s)
❏ Organization
❏ Job opening

More new contacts
❏ Organization
❏ Job opening

Basically, you can get an interview through the front door or the side entrance. Your résumé and cover letter are the "door openers" on cold calls, where no one at the organization knows you and you have not contacted anyone in advance. This is one tactic for getting interviews. The other tactic is to find someone who can refer you to an organization that you have identified and targeted or who can refer you to another organization that they are familiar with. That is the side door and the route for most hires.

Stepping-Stones—Friends, Family, Clients Equal Referrals

Consider the process of getting interviews as one that utilizes stepping-stones. In short—whom do you know who will be able to introduce you to someone in a company where you would like to work? Anyone you think would be willing to help is fair game. And, while we are on the stone metaphor, leave none unturned.

The Obvious Approach

The most obvious way to get an interview is ask for one. You send a letter inquiring about job opportunities. You follow up with a phone call. You ask for the interview, and you get it. Simple—would that it were so!

Think about it from the point of view of the people who agree to meet with you. If they agree to meet with you, they are also agreeing to take time away from something else—time not only for the meeting but also for all that is entailed in the preparation and the follow-up. Do not scrimp on time for courtesies, because they are always noticed even if you do not get direct feedback.

New Routes and Techniques

You need to use traditional approaches to get interviews, but you should also consider new routes and techniques as well. Use any method that gets you those interviews.

The Not So Obvious

The not so obvious opportunities are all those that do not immediately come to mind. In this situation, lists become important. For example, make a list of the various roles that you play (mother, father, neighbor, tennis player, soccer coach, church member, and so forth). Next name the people to whom you have the closest relationship in each role. Divide these people into three groups: The first group is made up of your fans. These people may or may not have job leads, but they will help you any way they can. The second group is (for whatever reason) nonfans, so they would need to be converted (a laborious and energy-consuming activity). The third group is made up of the unknowns. These are people you know, but you are uncertain if they are fans or not. From the first group, think about who may have leads for job interviews and openings. For example, in your role as soccer coach, you meet lots of other parents. Joe is a salesman and knows lots of people in different areas; maybe he knows someone in your field. Mary is a freelance programmer who has contacts at many different companies; maybe she knows of some openings.

Next take the list of contacts a step further. Who has jobs? Who knows people who have jobs? Who has contacts that could lead to interviews?

The Unusual

Do not ignore the people you see regularly but may have forgotten—the baby-sitter, the dog walker, your dentist, or your doorman. You deal with people who know a lot of other people; it does not hurt to ask if they have any information that might prove helpful. Even if they say no, they may run across something next week and remember your request.

The Outrageous

It is time to consider situations that you might never imagine as opportunities for effective networking. To get your creative juices flowing, you need to consider anyone from your past or present who, for whatever reasons, has caused you difficulty. Don't dismiss anyone too early. Ever get fired? Include those people who were directly responsible (without omitting those you suspect or were indirectly involved). Do not dismiss anyone who has affected you adversely. You need to consider the circumstances surrounding the difficulty and determine whether this person is a fan regardless of the circumstances and can this person help you either directly or indirectly to get a job.

Consider this example. An HR professional needed to replace a chief financial officer (CFO) in his organization, so he recommended to the owner that an executive recruiting firm be utilized and placed on retainer. His recommendation was accepted and the search was conducted successfully. The newly hired CFO quickly decided that the HR professional who had been responsible for his placement had to go because he represented competition for the owner's attention. When the time came for the CFO to make his recommendation, he also suggested that the recruiter

Role	Contacts
Roles You Play	

Roles You Play

List below all the roles you play.
List next to each role the names of all the people
you could contact to ask for job leads or interviews.

Role	Contacts

Mining Your Contacts

From the contact list on 2-2, choose those "fans" who may have job leads or contacts for you to follow up with.

Fans	Possible leads to:

who had recruited him be retained for the new search. Even though the recruiter accepted the task to recruit a replacement for the HR pro, he kept in touch and bore no ill will toward her. It turned out that she was a board member of several start-up firms. When one of them required a strong HR professional, she recommended the fellow who had been fired. The very important point to be made here is that when you network, look for your fans. The HR pro wisely understood that the recruiter would have been foolish to refuse an assignment because of loyalty to him. At the same time, by letting her know that he could use assistance (he had to ask), she indicated how much she valued his skills by recommending him to an organization in which she had a vested and economic interest—quite a compliment and an affirmation of her assessment of his professional skills.

Why Would Employers or Anyone Else Interview You?

❑ Friendship for you. You would do the same for them.

❑ You can add value. You can solve a problem.

❑ It makes them feel good to help others.

❑ It could make them look good to others; referring a great employee enhances their professional stature.

❑ Warding off evil. *"There but for the grace of God . . . ."*

❑ What goes around, comes around. You may be in a position to help them in the future.

❑ Respect for your referral.

❑ "No" is not in their vocabulary.

❑ They really do not have much else to do.

❑ They are always on the lookout for good people.

❑ They are flattered. *"Me? You think I am so powerful [insightful/plugged-in] that I can help you?"*

❑ Curiosity—they wonder what you have to say.

❑ *Hmmm. Do I know you? Are you someone I want to or should know?*

Why Should They See You?

This is the first question you need to address. If you don't find an answer, then you need to assume that no one should take the time to meet with you. And please do not say your reason is *"I need to network."* Before setting up meetings, you need to confidently determine what it is about you that is going to be of value to the person who has agreed to meet with you and with whom you wanted to meet. Remember you want the meeting because you feel that this person has the power, either directly or indirectly (he or she may refer you to someone who does have the power), to hire you. (Chapter 6 will help you to determine your core competencies and matching them to a targeted organization and job opening.)

"Why should someone interview you?" is a question that needs to be converted to *"Here's what I can do for you." "Here is the value I will add to the organization."* Or, *"You have this problem, and I offer this solution."* If you are looking for leads or further contacts, you have to then appeal to other reasons. *"I read an article that stated you were an expert in this field." "Susan Jones thought you would be helpful based on your experience." "Since you have just completed a successful job search, I was hoping you might give me some pointers on interviewing with XYZ Company."*

How to Approach Any Organization in the Hope of Getting an Interview

The next two questions should be reciprocal—*"Whom should be seeing you?"* and *"Who should you be seeing?"* Hopefully both parties are one and the same, but there are nuances to consider in order to maximize your time-effectiveness (and your chances for success). Expand your universe so that the circle of people you should be targeting becomes wider. This will make your job hunt more effective and increase your chances for success. By not doing this, you run the risk of cutting yourself off from those who are in a position to directly or indirectly be of assistance to you in your job search.

Who Should Be Seeing You?

The list of who should be seeing you includes the strongest to weakest (from the most to the least desirable):

❏ President, chief executive officer—more important than the head of the board of directors because this is the day-to-day leader of the organi-

Rules for Getting Interviews

1. Know and state your purpose. Be consistent and targeted with your résumé and marketing letter. Do you want a job, a lead, or guidance?

2. Do research. What do you know about the person, organization, or job opening?

3. Plan. Have an idea of what you will say and the questions you will ask. Be concise. Be prepared for both voice mail and a real person answering the telephone.

4. Ask outright, "*I am ____ and, I was hoping I could discuss ____ with you. Could you give me 5 [10 or 15] minutes?*"

5. Be flexible. If they cannot meet with you, would they be willing to spend a few minutes on the telephone with you? If this is not a good time, when would be better?

6. Be honest—if you want a job interview, ask. Do not pretend to seek advice when, in fact, you are fishing for job openings.

7. Let silence work for you. After you have stated your request, be quiet and wait for a response.

8. Be understanding. Is the person you called facing a big project? Just come back from vacation? Politely ask if you can leave your name and number? Could you check back in a week or so?

9. Be thankful—for whatever time they took out of their day, even if it was to say no.

zation. If you can get a response at this level, your résumé will get attention and at the very least get you a courtesy interview.

❏ Head of the board of directors—the same is true here, but this person is less likely to be as aware of the daily goings-on of the organization and not as in touch with needs and openings.

Bear in mind that just because you address your résumé to a senior level officer does not mean that will get VIP treatment. For example, there is a major entertainment company located in New York City that until recently had a president and CEO who sent every letter seeking a job to the chief counsel to whom human resources reported. This had the expected effect—HR would receive a letter with the stamps of the president and CEO and the chief counsel. Not knowing the nature of the contact, HR would follow up with the writer to determine whether to pursue the matter further. Recently, this time-wasting process was changed: Now all job-seeking letters go directly to HR unless the president and CEO know the applicant personally. In which case the résumé referrals continue to go to the chief counsel for review and further action. Notice though unless known to the president and CEO, all résumés are treated the same— unknown—by human resources. Résumés may also be routed to

❏ Other members of executive management.
❏ Other members of senior management (including HR).

It would be desirable for a job-seeking letter to be referred to any one of these executives because they are decision-makers. Remember the movie *Six Degrees of Separation?* The easiest route is always the one with the fewest steps, so whenever you get the chance to meet with one of these people you are definitely with one who has the power to offer you a job regardless of current openings.

Others connected to the organization that you should consider trying to contact are:

❏ Line managers
❏ Other employees
❏ Venture capitalists
❏ Consultants doing business with the organization
❏ Vendors doing business with the organization (including executive search firms and employment agencies the organization uses)
❏ Executive search and employment agencies the organization does not do business with
❏ Retired employees
❏ All other former employees
❏ Customers of the organization

Also consider using relatives of these people (for example, spouses and significant others) as a means of connecting you to these people. Think of them as being in "Tier 2," because in each of these instances it takes just two steps to get to the decision-maker.

Whom Should You See?

In a word, you should see anyone that either is relevant for your job
search prospects or will serve as an advocate or fan.

Ask yourself, who is the person that you will most likely be able to
sway? And who has the most power? Who will you probably see? In most
instances it comes down to whoever is willing to meet with you. Your need
to be practical and flexible—some would call this "playing the game"—is
the most important aspect of this process from your perspective.

Be sure to thank your contact person for his or her efforts in getting you
this invitation. If you don't meet with or get to see him or her for whatever reason, don't think that you must. This person got you in, so the only
thing you must do is remember to be grateful and send a thank-you note
by snail mail. Also bring your contact up to date as to whom you met with
and the results of the meeting.

Whom Will You Probably See?

A Subordinate to the Contact Person

How high up you reached in the organization to get your invitation will be
a factor in whether you meet the contact person or a subordinate. Don't be
disappointed if it's the latter, but give that person the same deference as
you would if you were meeting the original contact person. Subordinates
work alongside the person who had the interest and power to get you an
interview. By not appearing disappointed in meeting the subordinate, you
are demonstrating respect not only for the person you are dealing with but
for the superior as well. You may even find that the subordinate is easier
to deal with and may be a helpful contact (and more accessible) as you go
through the corridors of the organization.

The Human Resources Folk— Avoid Them at Your Own Peril

Sooner or later you will meet with a representative from the human resources department (or "people department" or whatever else the name
might be called in the organization). Do not avoid them or be disappointed when that happens. These folks aren't the old personnel paper push-
ers from the past. Most organizations have decided that since people are
more important to their organization's success than ever, those responsible for the recruitment and retention of employees have a most important

role in that process so the deadbeats or untrained don't get dumped there anymore. There are major attempts to attract a sharp bunch of people to this most important function.

Many career books make a point of advising job seekers to avoid human resources at all costs. Our advice is that to do so could be a huge mistake. The reason the warners are so emphatic is that their perception is that the folks in HR at their worst are bureaucratic and serve to impede everyone's candidacy and at their best have no power, so either way dealing with them is a waste of time. That still may be true if you are dealing with incompetent HR professionals or the organization you are dealing with still views the HR function as subordinate and administrative. HR professionals in whatever organization should be considered by you carefully because they are an indication of the way the organization values its human capital (yourself included) if you decide to join it.

What can HR do for you? Below is a list of activities the HR professional can perform on your behalf—all are essential to a successful organizational "landing."

1. HR can review your paperwork and forward it to the department with the job opening. For instance, HR plays an essential role in working with the hiring manager and the employment agency to make for fast turnaround time.
2. HR can prescreen you as an applicant.
3. HR can serve as your host.
4. HR can become your advocate.
5. HR can serve as your negotiator.
6. HR can help you to close the deal.
7. HR can serve as an organizational guide.
8. HR can continue to be an important contact as you move through the organization.

If you still need convincing, consider this summary of a situation that occurred recently in a major organization located in New York City. The HR recruiter working with line managers in public affairs offered a recent college grad a job as an administrative assistant with a base salary of $30,000. The applicant said she liked the organization, the job, and the people she would be working for but was having a difficult time rejecting another offer for $45,000. The recruiter spent the greater portion of the day working the phones with the line managers and the candidate to try to reach an acceptable compromise—and save the situation so that the organization was able to land a terrific candidate with enormous potential.

Oh, I Don't Know If It Is Worth
My While to Take This Interview

If you have the time, our advice is to interview rather than not. The major reason is that it is difficult to anticipate what the requirements will be when the interview actually takes place and you might find that the situation is better than you thought. The other reason is that the more you interview, the more proficient you become at it.

To e or Not to e?

Should you use the Internet to get interviews? We recommend that you use the Internet for its own sake, but as job strategy, it is there to use or ignore. Current studies show that only 4 percent of jobs are filled through the Internet. If there are 100,000 jobs available daily, then 4 percent would be the equivalent of 4,000 jobs. If you had those odds in the lottery, everyone would be a winner sooner or later. Don't spend too much time to the detriment of other sources (like networking), but try to mix your strategies so that you keep a fresh approach to each at all times.

Follow-up

Every person who has provided assistance to you in your search for leads and interviews deserves a thank-you note. If these people took time to consider you, you certainly can take the time to write a short note thanking them for their help and bringing them up to date on the status of the interview and your job search. Just because the lead they offered did not pan out, is no reason to not ask if they have thought of any other people or organizations that you could contact.

Questions

2.1 How can I help you?

Be ready for this one right out of the gate. You need a strong statement that exudes confidence and quickly gives the specific purpose for the phone call or meeting.

> *I seriously want to join XYZ Organization, and I could think of going to no one better than you to make my case.*

2.2 *What made you call me?*

> *I saw the interview you gave to the _____ Journal and your comments on the need for top talent to meet your biggest challenges. I thought I would volunteer to join the fight. Or You were listed in the Directory of _____ as the person responsible for _____. Since I too am interested in _____, I thought I would start with you.*

The point is to give a compliment to the person you are addressing with a strong statement rather than, *"To be completely honest, you were at the top of the alphabetical list so I thought I would start with you."*

2.3 *How did you get my number?*

This is an opportunity to tell the story and show that you have good research skills and persistence. Be careful, though, not to get anyone in trouble. Avoid a weak response such as, *"I called the general number and when I asked the switchboard operator who might be able to help, he gave me your name and number."*

2.4 *What makes you think you want to work in the _____ industry?*

This is something you should have covered as part of your research.

> *In considering my next career move, I started to read the state of technology in SAP applications. The more I read, the more I learned that XYZ is on the cutting edge and a global leader. The more I learned, the more I realized that this was the place for me. Furthermore, with my background in electrical engineering, I could make a real contribution on the hardware side.*

2.5 *What do you want to do for XYZ Company?*

Here you need to link what you specifically want to do with a position that the company has. Your research should have identified functional job titles that are specific to the company and the industry. If you want a job as a production assistant, be sure the company has such positions.

2.6 *What do you know about us?*

No excuse here for lack of preparation. Here is your chance to shine, but be careful not to blabber. Make a few statements that demonstrate you know who you are meeting with and then be quiet.

DSL.net is a leading provider of broadband Internet access for small- and medium-size businesses throughout the United States.

How do you get this kind of information? More often than not, you can get it from the organization's Website. However, if it doesn't have one, there is still no excuse for your saying you don't know anything about the company or assuming that because there is a dot between the "DSL" and the "net" that *". . . it has something to do with the Internet."*

2.7   Instead of coming to me, did you try calling the human resources department?

I thought of going to them, but I concluded that I'd prefer to come to you directly because it is you whom I was hoping I would get to spend a few minutes with. I felt you really have the challenge and would give me a short amount of time to determine whether we should spend more time getting to know each other better—if, that is, you conclude that I can be of assistance to you.

Flattery conveyed honestly and openly is very positive.

2.8   If I agree to a meeting, how much time will you need?

Whatever you do, refrain from saying, "Not much." Be specific. If you feel that 15 minutes is realistic and sufficient, say so and promise to stick to it. You might even add something humorous like—*"If I stay a minute longer, you can throw me out the door."* Understand, though, that you need to be out of there in less than 15 minutes because your honesty and your ability to keep your word are on the line. Of course, the person you are meeting with may want the meeting to run longer. Since you cannot be certain when this is the case, it is always a good practice to remind the person that you are ready to leave when your allotted time is up. If he or she wants you to stay, he or she will have to say so.

2.9   Why can't we do it over the phone?

Do not under any circumstances get argumentative here. You should be prepared for this question. Remember it was stated earlier that a case could be made for having the preliminary conversation over the phone. If you feel it is going well, then pause and suggest, *"I did not mean to take so much of your time. Might I suggest that we continue this conversation face-to-face? I promise to take no more than 15 minutes of your time."* On the other hand, if you are hoping for the name of a contact from him or her, men-

tion it. Before you make this call, you need to define what you want to result from it. If the prime purpose is a meeting, go for it. But if it is information you want, then ask for it. To be totally prepared, you should be
ready for both eventualities. Then be pleased that you achieved one of
your objectives—even if not the primary one. If you decided on only one
objective in advance and your request is refused, then you come away
with nothing.

2.10 *I really can't do it now. Why don't you try again in about 2 weeks?*

Here again, be gracious and let go but not before finding out if you can set
a date for the call or test the waters to see if you could have a brief meeting if that is what you prefer. Follow up with a thank-you note explaining
your purpose again. Include the date 2 weeks from the first conversation,
and if a specific time was agreed to, be sure to mention it as well. Then of
course be sure to make the call at the appointed time and date.

3

Technology, the Interview, and You

Whether you last searched for a job 25 years ago or 5 years ago, the current job market has changed substantially. Labor shortages exist in many business sectors and geographical areas. Registration for colleges is at an all time high. People remain working longer than they used to and may have five or six careers in a lifetime. "Casserole careers" are common, wherein workers have more than one job or career simultaneously. While some segments of the market are starved for employees, others are laying off workers and closing divisions. There also are continued shifts in the demand for labor as employers in the service industry continue to grow much faster than those in the manufacturing sector.

Jobs have changed. There are new jobs and new ways to do old jobs. A prime example is publishing, which moved from old printing presses to digital presses several years ago, thus turning an entire industry upside down. Now, the advent of E-books and E-publishing is changing it again. For example, Stephen King published a book solely online, and Fatbrain.com will list your manuscript on whatever subject you have written; readers can download your offering, for a price, if they wish. Electronic devices to read these electronic books are being streamlined, coming down in price, and many are looking to be the "next big thing." If the past 5 years seems to have brought about a world of differences, the next 5 will probably be even more volatile and filled with change.

It seems that with the coming of the millennium in January 2001, every magazine and newspaper, regardless of size or readership, prophesied about changes on the horizon as well as philosophized about the far and recent past. And the one statement on which there seems to be universal agreement is that change will always be with us and the rate of change continues to increase. Knowledge is the commodity of the moment—and of the future.

Going Digital

How widespread is the technological revolution? *WIRED Magazine's* Digital Citizen Survey (May 2000) estimated that only 23 percent of Americans are still not "wired"—that is, they do not identify any single piece of technology (cell or wireless phone, computer, Internet, E-mail, fax, online banking or investing, or online shopping) as playing an important part of their lives. Yet these self-confessed nonwired individuals also say that they are online with the Internet an average of 2 hours a week! Every week there are new ads placed everywhere except on people's foreheads for companies that we have never heard of—and most of them offer Websites. Innovations in technology—an entire wireless Web—are being made available to the global population.

How Many Careers Do You Have?
How many have you had? Where are you headed?

1. _____

2. _____

3. _____

4. _____

5. _____

6. _____

7. _____

8. _____

9. _____

10. _____

What Has Changed about the Job Search Process?

All this technology has given us cell phones, faxes, E-mail, the Web, and Personal Digital Assistant (PDA) devices. We can and do *"reach out and touch someone"* repeatedly every hour of the day. Not only are there smoke-free sections in restaurants, there are now "cell-free" areas. It is easier than ever to submit résumés. Résumés used to be called "the junk mail of the nineties." Now they are the Spam (spam is junk E-mail, unwelcome and unsolicited) of the millennium! The Internet and businesses are inundated with them.

Since it takes practically no time and actually no money, many job seekers E-mail résumés to more organizations than they would contact if it took more effort. This means that most of the résumés are often totally off the mark. The applicant has done little or no research; no visible effort has been made to target the job or the organization. No cover letter is even included. This is merely electronic mass mailing. The bulk of these candidates is clearly not a match for the stated job openings.

This scattershot approach *("Hey, you never know . . . maybe they have some kind of a job I could fill")* just overwhelms organizations. At the same time, the individuals reviewing résumés may be short on experience or on dealing with a new software HRIS (Human Resource Information System). Your painstakingly prepared résumé and marketing letter (if you took the time to submit one) may be opened and entered into the database by an inexperienced, poorly trained clerk or scanned in by text-reading software.

Technology is often used to screen the résumés submitted. Whether the résumé comes in as hard copy, as an E-mail, or as a document attached to an E-mail, many organizations have turned to an applicant tracking system (ATS) to scan and evaluate each résumé. If the résumé is not submitted in an ATS-friendly format, it may be ignored or coded by a clerk for submission to the database. This technology relies on key words being used on the résumé for the software to find the right one.

Another aspect of the tight job market is that there is considerable pressure on people in business to make the right hire because of all the effort and expense entailed in filling vacancies. Organizations may do more recruiting now than in the past to gather a pool of candidates to review. The ensuing selection process will include interviewing any likely applicants for comparison purposes.

Given all these filters and hurdles, if you are contacted for an interview, then you know that your résumé has survived a major sorting process. The interview becomes even more crucial. Even in a tight job market, more and more individuals are window shopping, that is, look-

---

Sample Electronic Résumé

Mary Jones
123 Main Street
Camp Hill, Pennsylvania 17012
212-787-6543
Msjones@internet.com
Http://JonesTV.xoom.com

KEY WORDS

Associate Director, 5-years' experience, relocate, Pennsylvania, Chyron Infinit, Quantel Picturebox, Quantel Paintbox, FAST VM Studio Editor, Sound Forge, Video Toaster 2000, Microsoft 2000 Suite (Word, Excel, PowerPoint), Photoshop, Illustrator, Image Composer, GIF Animator, FrontPage, entertainment industry, television, cable

CAREER OBJECTIVE

To obtain a dynamic position in the entertainment industry which offers opportunities for advancement and remuneration predicated upon abilities and effort

PROFESSIONAL EXPERIENCE

Lifetime TV for Women   1995 - Present

ASSOCIATE DIRECTOR

Assist the director during the course of the morning and evening newscasts
Coordinate remotes and live shots (obtain roll cues, traffic information, prep reporters for shots, act as liaison between location reporter and the show producer)

EQUIPMENT EXPERIENCE

Chyron Infinit
Chyron Maxine
Quantel Picturebox
Quantel Paintbox
FAST VM Studio Editor
Sound Forge
Video Toaster 2000

COMPUTER SKILLS

Microsoft Office 2000 Suite (Word, Excel, PowerPoint), Photoshop, Illustrator, Image Composer, GIF Animator, Front Page

EDUCATION

Cleveland State University, 1995, BA

Videotapes available on request

ing for one of those highly touted "big buck and lots of perks" jobs, so there are more and more résumés being floated about. There are thousands of résumés posted online with hundreds more added hourly. Some of these candidates are more or less serious about finding another job than you are. The one thing that you do not want to squander is this opportunity to sell yourself.

The Interview Itself Has Gone Techno

There are new types of interviews candidates are facing. New methods of determining the 'best' interviewee are being tried, such as the following:

❏ *Virtual interviews:* In these you sit in front of a computer monitor and keyboard. A small videocam is on top of the monitor. You are instructed to speak in a clear voice and to sit directly in front of the camera. The screen saver disappears, and your interviewer is online with you. The sound may or may not be clear. There may be image or sound distortion or timing differences between the image and the sound. You may lose the image or sound sporadically. On top of all the other elements being evaluated, your screen presence is now being evaluated!

❏ *Video interviews:* Think video dating, but these are for employers and employees looking for a match. Certain employment agencies allow applicants to record an interview session. Then employers can choose which videos to see based on résumés and other information on file at the agency.

❏ *Interactive interviews:* These may look like job application forms on the computer screen, but they serve as an interview method. Depending on how you respond to certain questions, you are asked for additional information or asked other questions. Again, it is not only your credentials that are being evaluated, but your keyboarding skills and ability to follow directions are being considered and may affect how you are assessed.

❏ *E-mail interviews:* These are like a take-home test, and they will be graded! You are E-mailed a questionnaire to complete and return. More than names and dates, interview questions are included. At least you get to mull them over. But, were those take-home tests in school really easy?

All Those Start-Ups! Good Deals versus New Deals

Depending on what the stock market is doing as you read this, the start-up dot.coms that have proliferated on the Internet as well as their multiple job openings will either still be around or not, or entirely new ones will have taken their place. The shelf life of these new business ventures has not been measured. In New York City alone, in April 2000 there were reported 8,000 new media companies employing 330,000 people.

In addition to unproven revenue streams and profits, these fledgling companies may not have invested much in the way of human resources. Programs, policies, and standards may be developed on a daily basis, as needed. Managers may more likely be technical geniuses or the most energetic entrepreneurs but not seasoned professionals in running a business. Managers in many of these organizations realize their lack of prowess in the day-to-day running of the business and seek to hire expertise ("gray-hairs" is the term bandied about for these elder hires). Ethics, morals, and working hours may run the gamut. Business and financial pressures—the need to succeed—will bring out either the best or the worst in their employees. The investors (either shareholders or venture capitalists) may have more of a say in the running of the organization than you had anticipated, or they may not continue their support when it's needed.

Working overtime and weekends may be the norm. Meeting deadlines while trying to conserve cash and hire as few employees as possible causes the few to do the work of the many. Additionally, management may have no idea what type of employees is needed or how many or when they should be hired. Do not stereotype these dot-com CEOs—they are not all brash, inexperienced "twenty-somethings." Many seasoned businesspeople are being enticed into the technology world, either starting their second (or third or fourth) career or expanding a brick-and-mortar business into one that is online.

Starting from scratch does not begin to describe some start-ups. Construction may be going on while you work. You may have to move into new quarters. Relocation may be delayed or put off indefinitely. The initial public offering (IPO) may not happen according to schedule or may be permanently delayed.

One good thing with all these ups and downs is that former employers are offering a type of amnesty to rehire their prodigal employees (all is forgiven—just come back). You cannot count on it though; for every employee who has profited financially by associating with a start-up, there are dozens who have not. *Fortune* magazine recently profiled three MBA grads who were each on their third dot.com company within a year! Being in on the start of a new venture can be exciting and a terrific learning experience; helping an organization grow can be particularly rewarding. A magazine article referred to these individuals starting up new businesses as "explorers," breaking into new frontiers. These explorers have permanently changed how the world and its employees do business.

Are You "Explorer" Material?

❏ What is your tolerance for risk? (Would you have been among the first Puritans to make the trip across the Atlantic Ocean?)

❏ Do you hunger for more routine in your professional life? Or less?

❏ Are you tired of attending endless and an infinite number of meetings?

❏ Do you thrive on uncertainty? Change?

❏ Do you want to supply more energy and find more excitement in your workday?

❏ How do you feel about 80-hour workweeks? Plus Saturdays and Sundays?

❏ Does your pulse quicken at the thought of quick riches and overnight fame?

❏ Do the trappings (first-class travel, car service, offices with appropriate furniture) of the traditional organization bore you?

❏ Do you feel you could live and thrive in an environment without structure where process is viewed as an untried and unnecessary element?

❏ Will you survive and thrive in a place where there are no rules, or you make up the rules as you go along?

❏ How comfortable do you feel making rapid decisions based on limited information? Constantly resetting priorities to adjust to endlessly changing marketplace demands?

What Should You Know about a Start-Up?

Barry Diller, the chairman of USA Networks, warns *"Try not to work with a company run by 25-year-olds, no matter how smart they are, because they are essentially in their first jobs."* (*PC Week*, March 6, 2000, page 9)

What is your tolerance for dealing with people younger than yourself? That is the first fact of life whether it is a dot.com or any other start-up that you need to deal with.

Do you need to be respected? Employees who brought the organization to where it is when you enter the picture won't be too deferential since they are probably part owners.

Are you ready to help do whatever needs to be done? Find talent? Stuff envelopes? Proofread ad copy? Help to find real estate and telephone systems—in a word, jump in, roll up your sleeves, and do whatever needs to be done at the moment?

What are the finances? Do you know who is supplying the funds? What are the terms of the financing? Are there strategic partners involved? Is an IPO planned?

Do you understand what the start-up's mission is and how it is going to be accomplished? What is its product? Would you buy what it is selling? Do you understand it? Make sure you understand it so well that you are able to explain it to someone else.

You owe it to yourself to do your research. Find out what the competition is. What are the risks of the product? the industry? Would you invest your own money in this company?

Evaluate the managers? What is their history? Their background? Are they knowledgeable? Ethical? Not just bright, but smart as well? What about the employees? Are they ready to delegate, or do they only want a bunch of clerical assistants?

How do they spend money? Is the office appropriate for the business that is being conducted there? If the office decor reminds you of a major investment bank or Gordon Gekko's offices in *Wall Street*, then they may be spending their money on the wrong priorities.

What are the work habits of the people (including the founders) who are already there? Is the atmosphere chaotic or productive? Pleasant and high in energy or more of a boiler room setting with a lot of tension in the air? Would they think you are less than loyal if you go home earlier than nine in the evening and do not want to be called at home under any circumstances? Remember this is their baby. You need to go through a baptism of fire if it is to be your baby, too.

Are they going public? What is their attitude about that? Are they giving too much attention to the public offering and getting distracted from the reason for being there in the first place?

Last, because it is a start-up, accept the fact that the chances of success and the risk of failing are both high.

Questions

3.1 *What experience do you have with start-up situations?*

More than once, I've had responsibility for working with the team responsible for setting up a new business unit for _____ corporation when the company went through rapid growth. I think those experiences will be applicable here. And because of them, I will hit the ground running.

3.2 *The average age of our employees is ____ years. How would you manage them?*

I've had a lot of experience both as coach for the local _____ team and manager at XYZ Corporation with managing employees who were a variety of ages. I have found there are similarities (like being fair and consistent) and differences (like speaking in a language they understand) that have made me an effective manager. I will be effective here taking that same approach.

3.3 *How flexible are your working hours?*

I realize this is a start-up, so I understand that I need to be as flexible as the situation requires. If I did not understand the time demands and agree to them beforehand I would not be here talking to you about this opportunity today.

3.4 *How do you feel about filling in, as needed, in other jobs?*

It goes with the requirements of a start-up. You do whatever is required. When I was in the TV industry and we were shooting on location, you did whatever the situation demanded. The same will be true here. It is an exciting challenge and one in which I will never be bored.

3.5 *What do you think our No. 1 priority should be?*

Not to sound presumptuous but if I had to say, from what I have learned thus far, the No. 1 priority should be to have the best individuals in the required slots as quickly as they are needed.

3.6 How do you deal with ambiguity?

I face it directly to get as focused a picture as I can. Then I remind myself to stay flexible and as soon as I receive or observe anything that alters that picture, I make the adjustment and refocus to see what impact that has on any activities planned to start in the near future or already under way.

3.7 Do you like to get your hands dirty?

I don't mind at all, because it's a good way to stay connected. In the army I learned that the great leaders were the ones who didn't ask their troops to do anything they wouldn't. That same principle should apply and be quite effective here as well.

3.8 Over the next year, we all will be working under pressure to meet deadlines. Can you commit to support our efforts?

I realize that you need someone who is going to be available for anything that appears on the radar screen, and that means making this my No. 1 priority for the foreseeable future. You can count on me.

3.9 If necessary, can you relocate?

Just give me warning and provide assistance with the arrangements, and I'll go wherever you require me to be.

3.10 Are you available for extensive travel?

As I mentioned before, if you offer me the job, this organization will be my first priority on a 24/7 basis, so just let me know what you need me to do and where you need me to be, and I will be there ready to go.

3.11 We are working on our mission statement. What do you suggest should be included?

I would appreciate spending more time with you before I would presume to say anything, but if you press me to say what it should include, from what I have heard so far, I recommend that the mission statement make a direct statement indicating the importance of the customer, the stakeholders, and the employees—as well as the organization's commitment to excellence.

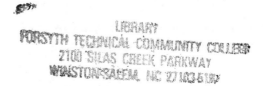

4
What Hasn't Changed?

Employers are still looking for the same qualities in a new hire that they have always sought. Over the last 10 to 20 years, most employers have realized—as have most employees—that the ideas of a "job for life" and "permanent hires" are pretty much concepts of the past (although some millennium predictions include a return of employer/employee loyalty). Employees pick up and leave very easily, with little or no effect on their ability to land another job; being able to telecommute has shattered geographic boundaries. Casual Fridays have expanded into casual clothing all week long in some places. In fact, now there is a move (spearheaded by some clothing manufacturers) to have "dress-up Thursdays"!

Consumers are being upset with the lack of quality in products and especially in services; complaints are overwhelming, particularly on the Internet. Organizations are beginning to listen and are marketing their products differently as well as reconsidering the products they are marketing.

Employers, ever cost-conscious, carefully consider every hire more comprehensively than ever. They know the costs of finding and training a replacement that is needed because of a "bad" hire. In a tight job market, recruiters reach into organizations to find new candidates, so employers want to attract and keep the best. Finding the best has always been the key.

So what is the interviewer hoping to find? *Can do, will do, fit!* They want a candidate who will be "their kind of people" with the motivation and the skills to meet the goals and objectives of the job and the organization.

How is the candidate assessed for these qualities? The first tests are the résumé and marketing letter. Was the candidate a referral? If so, by whom? Since you, the job seeker, target the organization and the position, your first hurdle in getting the interview is seeing how well you have done with your résumé and letter.

The hiring manager, based on what he or she is reading, must be able to start to envision you in the job. The reader must be intrigued—the reader must want to know more. He or she must want to meet you. Do not forget, the reader *wants* to want you for the position. A quick, correct hire saves organizations a lot of time and effort. If you have piqued their interest, correctly targeted the specific organization, and have matched your "solution" to their needs, they will more likely contact you for an interview.

Another element many organizations look for is *risk-taking*. This does not refer to a financial manager who goes to Las Vegas with the 401K funds! They want people who can think "out of the box." That is someone who thinks "the way we always did it is best" or "that's the way so and so always insisted we do it" is not the way to think anymore. New very different times demand state of the art, creative ideas. Thinking beyond a narrow focus is to think outside the boundaries of the specialist mindset or "out of the box." Business is changing rapidly; technology is driving the change in many cases. Competition is global. Organizations are not as interested in 15 years of the same experience as they are in 5 years of changing, evolving experiences.

Organizations need both *learners* and *teachers*. Which are you? New organizations not only need new talent with new ideas and new ways to do things, but they are also realizing the need for depth in management and experience. "Gray-hairs," mentioned earlier, is the term used when organizations seek to hire those seasoned employees who have "been there, done that" to provide the business sense needed to apply new ideas. Are you a good teacher? A fast learner? How well do you learn from others? How do you determine what you need to know and where can you obtain the required information or skill? How able are you to share what you know in an effective manner?

Loyalty versus slaves—is there a fine line? The stories are legendary of younger employees who are willing to work 10- to 14-hour days, 7 days a week to get ahead. How willing are you? Then there are other stories of executives, in the prime of their careers, dropping out and taking low-profile jobs so that they can spend more time with their families. Job sharing, flextime, and telecommuting are also signs that workers' relationships with their employers are changing. Compared with the job for life outlook of 10 to 20 years ago, these are radical changes. It is not unusual for a person to have five to six different careers, let alone different employers, in a lifetime. It may not be a question of the right job as much as a job for right now for many job seekers. Each position may be viewed as a stepping-stone on a long-range path to an ultimate career. What is your attitude toward employment and commitment to employers? What do you think their commitment to you as an employee should be?

What Is Your Profile?

Indicate where you fit on the following criteria.

1 = does not fit me at all   2 = fits me seldom   3 = fits me sometimes
4 = fits me most of the time   5 = fits me perfectly

			What level do you think the job requires?
Risk-taker	1 2 3 4 5		_____ ?
Learner	1 2 3 4 5		_____ ?
Teacher	1 2 3 4 5		_____ ?
Loyalty	1 2 3 4 5		_____ ?
Commitment	1 2 3 4 5		_____ ?
Extrovert	1 2 3 4 5		_____ ?
Introspection	1 2 3 4 5		_____ ?
Leader	1 2 3 4 5		_____ ?
Follower	1 2 3 4 5		_____ ?
Team-builder	1 2 3 4 5		_____ ?
Flexibility	1 2 3 4 5		_____ ?
Live to work	1 2 3 4 5		_____ ?
Work to live	1 2 3 4 5		_____ ?

Intangibles

There are other qualities, just as important as those skills and experiences highlighted on your résumé and in your marketing letter, that are looked for in an interview because employers value them in employees. One critical quality is *credibility*. This is why interviewers ask so many questions about your background—to see how you react in different situations and to find out what your experiences have been. This is another reason why body language, tone of voice, and presentation skills are so important in an interview. Are you to be believed? You are not merely selling your candidacy, you are conveying your credibility. When you say that you can do the job, can you be believed?

Reasons Candidates Needlessly "Fail" Interviews

What could *you* do to not commit these interviewing errors?

- ❏ Lateness
- ❏ Tactlessness
- ❏ Passivity and indifference
- ❏ Too much interest in money
- ❏ More interest in IPO prospects than the business
- ❏ Preoccupation with benefits
- ❏ Lack of eye contact
- ❏ Weak handshake
- ❏ Sloppy or poor appearance
- ❏ Lack of preparation
- ❏ Poor speaking skills
- ❏ Lack of manners
- ❏ Nervousness
- ❏ Lack of planning or goals
- ❏ Immaturity
- ❏ Evasive responses
- ❏ Résumé details different from application and/or interview statements
- ❏ Negative statements about supervisors and/or employers
- ❏ Expectations too high
- ❏ Inflexible expectations
- ❏ Arrogance
- ❏ Lack of interest in organization or job
- ❏ Sloppy application form
- ❏ Just a feeling or general impression, "I don't know why"
- ❏ Sarcasm
- ❏ Lack of attentiveness
- ❏ Strong prejudices
- ❏ Looked different on paper
- ❏ Overstated qualifications
- ❏ Came in under false pretenses
- ❏ Unwilling to give references
- ❏ Poor references

Or will you invent a new one?

Another intangible that the interviewer will try to assess is *enthusiasm.* Most candidates will muster some eagerness for the position in the interview, but which ones are truly enthusiastic? Most interviewers equate enthusiasm in an interview with motivation. Interviewers know that there may be other positions that you are actively considering, so how can they measure how sincere you are about working for them (versus just getting a job)? One measure is how much effort you have put into the interview through research. Do you know about the company, its products, its history? Do you even know what industry it is in? Are you just window-shopping, or are you sincerely interested in making a career move to this organization? If so, why? You need to have strong answers to these questions, even if they are not asked directly.

Typical Subjects for Interview Questions

Basically, if it is in your résumé—or obviously missing from your résumé—it is fair game. If you are asked to fill out a job application, which typically goes into greater detail than most résumés, the information you provide is a basis for further discussion. Do not ignore or forget what you said in your cover letter. (You kept a copy to refer to, right?) as well as what you mentioned over the telephone or in your E-mail.

These are the categories typically explored in an interview:

❑ **Education:** where, what, why, and with whom? What have you learned lately? What are you learning now?

❑ **Work history:** who, what, when, where, why, and for how much pay? Has there been a plan? Do your jobs show progression? Promotions?

❑ **Skills:** what, when, where, and to what degree of expertise? Are yours the skills we need now? How are you keeping up to date?

❑ **Experience:** where, when, and how related to current position? Can you apply here what you have learned and done elsewhere? Can you teach others?

❑ **Personal:** Who are you? What are your interests, goals, strengths, weaknesses, plans, aspirations, failures, and achievements? Do you want to join us? Can we believe you?

❑ **Marketing package:** What exactly are you selling? Why are you selling to us? What can you do for us? How much will you cost? Do we need you and your skills? How can we best use you?

❏ **The organization and the job:** Who we are, how we work, our mission, job requirements, job potential, and problems.

Do some of these topics leave you less than comfortable? Do you have skeletons in your closet? Insecurities and regrets can surface during an interview; face them ahead of time and plan how you will discuss them.

For example, for financial reasons, you were unable to attend what some might term a "prestigious" college or university. You attended a local community college and finally continued your studies and graduated at a state college. Not being able to go to school full time and have the college experience has always been a sore point with you. How will you answer the question, *"Why did you go to school there? Why did it take you 6 years to graduate?"*

Strengths and Weaknesses—What Are Yours?	
For your own review, list your top five weakest and strongest areas to discuss in an interview.	
Weakest areas	**Strongest areas**
1.	1.
2.	2.
3.	3.
4.	4.
5.	5.

You can assume that the topics listed above will be covered, so be prepared. The trick in each interview is how this information will be obtained. How will the questions be framed, and what is the agenda of the interviewer? The interviewer's style must also be considered; as the interview proceeds, you can see what style is evident.

No matter what, these facts hold true:

❏ The candidate must help the interviewer come to the right decision about his or her candidacy by establishing rapport with the interviewer. This rapport will allow both the candidate and the interviewer to complete their agendas in the meeting.

- ❏ Good manners are always appreciated; bad manners (or total lack of them) are always noticed.
- ❏ Interviews all have a beginning, a middle, and an end; it is the mutual responsibility of both the candidate and the interviewer to make the most of each step of the process.

Interviewer's Approach

- ❏ **Question and answer:** Primarily a back-and-forth type of interview. Format can be either structured or unstructured.

  Closed-ended questions require a simple yes, no, or I do not know. These types of questions do not elicit or allow for much interaction or discussion.

  Open-ended questions practically demand the respondent to elaborate, and the response may be more than was intended. These are the questions that are often answered with too much information. Take a moment, if needed, to consider your answer; give your response and be quiet. Let the interviewer speak next. If silence continues, consider asking, "*Did I answer your question?*" "*Was that sufficient information?*" or "*Do you need additional details?*"

- ❏ **Lectures:** Interviewer talks more than listens. Gets involved in own stories, anecdotes, and explanations. You may not be able to tell your story, but, if you are a good listener, you may still be recommended for the job.

- ❏ *Discussion:* Questions lead to discussions of issues and each side is represented fairly. Both parties are permitted to take turns as speaker and listener.

- ❏ **Stress:** Uses silence mercilessly. Favorite may be an accusatory "*Why did you (or didn't you) . . . ?*"

- ❏ **Passive:** Expects candidate to do all the talking. "*Tell me about yourself*" is the major thrust of questioning.

- ❏ **Combination of any of the above**.

❑ The positive thought, *"I will succeed because I believe I will succeed"* can carry a candidate through tough interviews.

❑ Being physically and mentally fit is a requisite for interviewing. Feeling good about yourself and being alert are assets that sell well in any interview situation.

❑ Although occasionally interviews are adversarial or unpleasant, the majority of interviewers want you to be the candidate to hire—it solves their immediate problem.

Questions

4.1 Are you a people person?

Do not assume that this question comes from a friendly direction. The interviewer may perceive you as a "softy" and therefore considers you apt to respond very positively to this question. When you do she or he will bury you alive. Better to present yourself (and practice too) in a balanced approach that emphasizes both people or tasks based on the situation.

I am a results person and will do what the situation requires to achieve goals—be they quality, timeliness, cost-effectiveness, or all of the aforementioned. I realize that people are needed to hit goals and objectives, but I am not there to be their buddy. However, I would be doing them and the organization a disservice if I did not work with them effectively.

4.2 Are you considering other positions at this time?

This question has always been a favorite. For the first-time job seeker, be careful to demonstrate that you are really focused and not considering jobs that vary in range from teaching through park ranger with auto assembly worker in between.

I am also considering a similar position with the LMN company, your competitor.

This brief answer shows that you are very focused. Simply put, you really know what you want and you understand the industry.

Quite frankly though, I really would rather work for (the name of organization you are meeting with) because it clearly is the leader (or No. 2 in the industry).

There are arguments for wanting to be with No. 2, and here is the place to make them.

4.3 *Describe a typical day.*

Watch out for this "gimme." It is like one of those slo-mo pitches that seems as if you will have to wait all day to hit but in fact it could really be a trap if you are not prepared. Be brief and really shine by emphasizing activities that show a bias for action, the need for very little supervision, and demonstrated results.

My day starts with my arrival at 7:45. First thing I do is check my voice mail and then review my E-mail to be sure that there are no crises that need immediate attention. Then I review my list of things that I need to do that day (including a review of my calendar) and proceed to attack the most challenging item on the list. I then start to review any mail and return phone calls. When 9 o'clock comes, we have a brief staff meeting to be sure everyone is aware of what occurred the day before and what needs to be done that day. At the first opportunity I check in with my supervisor to be sure she is informed of what is going on and to see if she needs me for anything. The rest of the day I spend roaming around to see what is going on, attending meetings that require my presence, and solving problems as quickly as they occur. Weekly I meet with each of my direct reports to be sure that each is meeting objectives and accomplishing results.

4.4 *Describe three things that are important to you in a job.*

In any job I take, my top three musts include a great organization, a product or service in which I truly believe, and a real career opportunity.

It is as simple as that. Whether you deviate from the statement written here or not, be sure to practice making your statement in advance of the interview to a friend or colleague because the more prepared you are, the more confident you will sound when you actually make the statement in the interview.

4.5 *Do you know anyone who works here or used to work here?*

From the interviewer's point of view, this gives her or him the opportunity to "check you out" with someone known to the organization and whom the organization knows. The interviewee immediately goes from the unknown to a known quantity. "Like attracts like" is the saying that you as the interviewee are interested in applying here. This may also relate to treatment toward you. You should know the answer to this question before going in, because you should be going to people you know as part of your research.

4.6 *Have you seen our advertising? Our commercials? What did you like or not like about them?*

Advertising, TV commercials, and any other image opportunities the organization conveys should be observed by you as part of your preparation and research before the interview. Not only does the organization pay to portray itself in a specific manner, but by selecting this product or service and spending money to promote it reveals the organization's priorities at this time to the exclusion of other products and services that are not getting promoted. Then there are layers of understanding too that must be considered when an organization chooses humor, for instance, to convey its message. Such matters should be considered in advance of the interview so that you can demonstrate your awareness and discuss them intelligently if the opportunity arises.

4.7 *Have you seen or used our product(s) or service(s)? What did you like or not like about them?*

It may not be possible in every instance for you to use the products or services of the organization you are meeting with. Nonetheless, there is no excuse for not being familiar with them and speaking knowledgeably when the opportunity arises. Ideally, if you can put the product or service to use, do so. That goes also for the interview itself. When you are meeting with the folks that make Snapple, don't ask for a Coke when they ask if they can get you a beverage. Whether it is the WWF or Lifetime TV, if you want a job in either organization, it just isn't effective to say *"My spouse watches your programs all the time."* The implication is *". . . but I don't."*

4.8 *How am I doing as an interviewer?*

Everyone likes feedback, including interviewers. You might turn it around and say,

> *You look like you really enjoy this. Have you been interviewing for a long time?*

If you feel comfortable you might even take this opportunity to inject a question that you wanted to be asked.

> *If the roles were reversed, the only question I might have asked is "_____."*

4.9 *How are you doing?*

This basic question is a friendly gesture asked to see if you are holding up okay. Your physical appearance may be raising the question, so take a quick inventory. If you need a glass of water, say so. If you are not feeling well, use this opportunity to excuse yourself if you need to.

4.10 How did you learn about our organization? How did you get information about us?

This is a nice opportunity to show how well you have done your homework. Don't blow it by going on and on. You don't need to show everything you did. Pick your response:

The Internet and your Website were both really helpful.

I called your investor relations department and the person I spoke with was really helpful.

I saw in The Wall Street Journal *that you utilize the services of the public relations firm, _____. So I called there, and it was really helpful.*

4.11 How do you establish rapport with clients and coworkers?

From the start, I exude confidence and respect for them as professionals and colleagues. I take every opportunity to include them in every relevant conversation or keep them up to date afterwards. I speak with them frequently and look for opportunities to share information. I also make a point of providing feedback on as frequent a basis as the situation allows—I prefer doing this face to face. Phone calls are second best. E-mail is a help as the third option because it serves as a written record of what has taken place. Also as a feedback mechanism, it is so easy and immediate to tell someone "nice job" or "it will be taken care of right away" in response to a memo from a coworker or request from a client.

4.12 How do you establish your credibility?

Careful listening and a professional bearing are the key elements in setting the right tone from the start. Then I look for opportunities with a fast return and good visibility where I can truly add value to the situation. I don't worry about how senior the request is but rather how receptive the person who has the issue or problem will be to my involvement. I try to not overpromise, but I do try to overdeliver. From the start, I pay attention to the details and evaluate the strengths and weaknesses of those I am dealing with directly as well as those around that person. For example, I don't want to get into a finger-pointing situation when an assistant mistakenly scheduled an appointment. I would rather make sure that the assistant had the date right from the start so that we can all look good all the time.

4.13 How do you get people to open up?

People love to be recognized and appreciate the chance to talk about themselves. By slowly and gradually showing that you genuinely care for each of the people you have to deal with, you will not only get them to open up but, more importantly, you will get them to respond and assist you whenever the situation calls for it. When I was at XYZ Company as a temporary employee, I made a point of getting to know the people in the mailroom and at the switchboard so that if anyone was looking for me—whether in person, over the phone, or through the mail—these people would know exactly who I was and where I was located. They were all so delighted that I paid attention to them that I think they were more responsive to me than to other employees who were there as permanent workers. As a result, I knew about the proud garden of one of the switchboard operators and all about the vacation trip to the Caribbean for another. And I never lost a phone call or a piece of mail that was supposed to go to me in the 2 months I was there.

4.14 How do you like to be managed?

This is a self-interest question for the hiring manager who is asking it.

I take a plain and simple approach to work. Let me know what needs to be done, and let me show what I can do. If I have any problems, I will bring them to your attention as soon as they arise if I am unable to solve them first on my own. Additionally, if there is anything that I learn that is a "need to know" for you while I am accomplishing my tasks, I will pause to bring the matter to your attention. Please feel free to comment. I would like to know your thoughts.

What manager will fail to be impressed with this brief, targeted response?

4.15 How do you set your personal priorities?

My personal priorities should begin and end with my supervisor. I start by drafting my own list. Once that is done, ideally I would meet with my supervisor. I then see what his or her needs are and include them on the list. Then I review the revised list to ensure that my revised list is in sync with his or her requirements and priorities. Is this how you expect your subordinates to operate?

4.16 How do you think this interview is going so far?

If you feel it is going well, say so, but add *"what do you think?"* If you have doubts, this is the right time to try to revive the meeting. A weak response would be *"I must admit I am a bit frustrated because I feel I have not been effective thus far."* A better response would be:

As long as you give me the opportunity to show how I could add value quickly and directly to your department before the end of the interview, I will say the interview is going quite well so far. Do you feel the same?

4.17 *How much supervision do you feel you require?*

Hiring managers are really hoping to hire employees who will manage themselves so that they can give their attention to all the other things they have going on. You can really take a big lead over other candidates if you let the interviewer know in no uncertain terms that you require little if any supervision.

> *I am a "low-maintenance" person who will always be sure you are up to date and informed about any activities I am performing that require your attention or approval. It is more likely that you will come looking for me to either bring something to my attention or assign something else to me rather than me seeking you out to solve my problems.*

4.18 *How would you convince one or more coworkers that your way of doing something is better than the current way?*

> *I would start the conversation by letting them know that I am interested in hearing their opinion on a matter I am about to bring to their attention. Then I would state the subject and ask them for the background as to the current procedure being followed. I would listen very carefully. Then I would offer my suggestion briefly, and then I would be quiet. I would listen to see what the objections are, if any. I would then evaluate the points mentioned. If their concerns are valid, I would thank them and reconsider the procedure. If I still felt that my suggestion was an improvement, I would ask them if they would try my suggested procedure for a short time and see if it works. We would then talk about it and see what changes needed to be made to the procedure. We would draft the procedure together.*

4.19 *Identify a safety problem you faced and explain how you dealt with it.*

> *When I first arrived in my unit, I was appalled to see broken furniture along the back wall. I lost all patience about a half hour later when I was escorted into the conference room. I tried to sit in the chair closest to me and was stopped by at least three people warning me that the chair was broken. Right then and there I got a representative from facilities on the phone and instructed him to remove all the broken furniture from our unit as soon as possible. In front of everyone, I asked when it would be accomplished and then told all my subordinates this was going to be our procedure for all broken furniture. And I reminded them of the safety issues involved.*

4.20 *If you are hired, what would be the first thing that you would do?*

You want to take this opportunity to remind the interviewer that if she or he hires you, you would be with her or him from the start.

I would sit down with you and take careful notes while you were telling me what your priorities are and briefing me on any other matters that you feel warrant my attention.

4.21 Sell me this pen/watch/book/chair.

This is a traditional request that really is a work sample test if you are being considered for a selling position. Start with a question that pulls the interviewer in, and then take it from there.

Are you thinking, "Oh no, not another pen salesperson!"? Just what I suspected. This is not "another pen." It is the only pen that you will ever need. What is your biggest annoyance with pens these days? Mine too.

Or if none could be thought of, suggest the following:

Let me tell you what I hear from so many others (list three). This pen will eliminate that (those) problem(s) with its _____ and make you feel that writing is a real pleasure again. Now you may think a pen like this will cost your organization 15, 20, even 50 cents each, but just because we want you to try it with no strings attached we will make it available to you for only 7 cents, and just see the requests come in for more. Everyone will think you are the hero because you found 'em. Let me just pull out this purchase order . . . .

What you have done is attracted the attention of the interviewer (gotten the interviewer involved) demonstrated listening skills, addressed the interviewer's need, asked for the sale, and finally closed the sale—all within 30 seconds.

4.22 Tell me about a personnel problem you have solved.

When I first took responsibility for my unit, we had a real tardiness problem. I knew it because the time sheets were on my desk. I saw two problems—first, the rampant tardiness and, second, the time sheets on my desk. I quickly decided to try a new procedure. I appointed one of the administrative assistants as the attendance clerk and gave her the responsibility for the time sheets. I sensed she was one of those people who have this sense of fairness and justice. And she also happened to like to come in early, read the paper, and have her breakfast before the day started. She was also an informal leader. No one complained about her new responsibility, and the problem disappeared immediately. It is amazing how appointing a key person makes the lateness problem go away. Employees have to be truthful with time sheets and will begin to feel guilty about being late. They will have a problem when arrival and departure times are recorded accurately.

4.23   *Tell me about a technical problem you have solved.*

When I first got to XYZ Company, there was no up-to-date telephone direc-tory. Facilities had responsibility for it, but did not make it a priority. One of the executive assistants had made her own directory on two sides of a sheet of paper. She offered to let human resources distribute it to everyone, but she also wanted to stop being responsible for it. The only other problem was that the company had gotten so big that her two-sided sheet didn't work anymore. I approached one of the administrative assistants who was very proficient with word processing, and she solved the problem quickly and effectively.

4.24   *What can you tell me that I do not already know that would make me hire you?*

Be deliberate with your answer. Take the challenge and run with it. Chances are this is a wind-down question, and the interviewer has al-ready made up his or her mind, so do not be worried about blowing it with your answer here. If you haven't been successful already and gained a fan, the interviewer will not be converted here. Be brief and profession-al with your answer. Also this is the time to mention anything that you feel you should have but did not have a chance to discuss until now.

You seem to be having a problem with _____. Is that correct? With my ex-perience in the field and working at NOP Corporation which had a similar problem, I will be able to quickly prove my worth.

Or

It sounds as if you need someone right away. Am I correct? I want this job so much that even though I have plans to spend a few days at _____, I would cancel them so that I could be here right away.

4.25   *What are three qualities that have contributed toward your success and three that you must work on?*

This is a difficult question because you are not asked to name one but three positives and three negatives (although the interviewer is astute enough not to use the word). Your response should be brief. The three positives are easy enough but stay brief and focused.

My sharp listening skills, an appealing leadership style, and a bias toward ac-tion are three very helpful positives.

If you want to play it safe, you could pick those same three and give negative aspects.

My sharp listening skills are quick to help me to remember the commitments people make to me. When they don't deliver and I remind them, I could do this more diplomatically. My appealing leadership style doesn't work on those who view that style as a weak one. I need to start more aggressively with those who challenge my leadership when they arrive. The bias toward action sometimes means a swift response, which may be less effective than if the situation had been better researched initially.

4.26 What business are we in?

There is no excuse for being unprepared for this one. Nothing is worse than not knowing what product the organization you are meeting with produces. However, sometimes it is harder and harder to tell. If it is a publicly held company, get the annual report and check out recent press releases to make sure they have not redefined themselves. If it is privately owned, do a search on the Web, and as part of that search find out if the organization has its own Website. If it does, be sure to visit it. In the not-for-profit sector, your best bet again is the Web.

4.27 What do you think is our organization's strength? Weakness?

Here is your chance to show what separates this organization from its competition. If you did your research and listened carefully to the organization's interviewers, chances are they provided some clues.

We are a 6 sigma organization. We are ISO 9000 certified. We are always striving to be best in class.

When competitors are named, remember the reason—chances are it is for comparison purposes. Remember the details. See what the press says. When it comes to mentioning any weakness, be brief and try to single out something that you already know is in the process of being fixed. First Union, for instance, closed the Money Store after it paid $2 billion for the acquisition. Nortel went to outsourcing to allow its energies to stay concentrated on its core businesses.

4.28 What do you think it takes to be successful in a business like ours?

Don't go wild with business school models, as tempting as the situation might be. Instead stick to basics—great people is a safe one; technology is a second; research and development, a third. Then show how any will be the catalyst. By keeping it at a basic level, you are not avoiding the question entirely (*"I can't really say for sure until I get an insider's view . . . ."*) and you are not saying that the answer is so simple, you wonder why the organization hadn't already seen it. Any organization can make a difference depending on the group of people it is able to attract, retain, and motivate. For example, if the organization is technology-dependent, then technology is the engine that should drive the organization to success. When Polaroid was foundering, in a brainstorming session the suggestion was made to develop an instant, throwaway camera. Polaroid already had most of the technology and research and development, so it put together the rest and its revival is assured, at least for the short run.

5

What Is New in the Workplace?

It is not just new products, new ideas, and new ways of doing things; the workplace itself is new for many employees. Changes in the work environment have driven changes in what employers look for in new hires. For example, changes in technology have triggered changes in ideas. *"If we are planning on doing things differently, should we not rethink exactly what we are doing and why?"* Rather than reinventing the wheel, many are looking at the wheel itself to determine if it is needed and, if so, how it best can be used.

It is a myth that workers used to have only one employer for life; 20 years ago less than 8 percent of male workers in the private sector had worked at the same company for 25 years. Studies conducted during the year 2000 indicate that the average middle-aged worker will spend less than 8 years at the same company. Do the math: if workers continue to work longer, past traditional retirement age, how many employers will each of these workers have? Turnover is a fact of life at organizations and management must deal with hiring, training, and financial fallout.

Test Drives

The increased demand for knowledge workers has seen some movement toward "try before you buy" by employers. How does an employer know who can really deliver what is promised, particularly in technology-based workplaces? Work samples and portfolios can only go so far. Some employers want to do more than kick the wheels—they want a test drive. Interviewers may pose case study questions or technical "what ifs" to test your knowledge as well as your thinking skills. How can you prove your technical expertise in an interview?

A Look into the Future Workplace

❏ Any place can be a workplace and any time can be "office hours." Home, office, and anywhere in between will all be acceptable for working.

❏ With the variety of places to work, family and women-centered businesses will become more prominent.

❏ Sizes of organizations will be more fluid. Staff will have to become flexible to all these changes.

❏ Workers will be owners. Employees will look to own a piece of the action through options or stock ownership.

❏ Since buying in to companies will become more prevalent, loyalty will return.

❏ School-to-work arrangements will increase. Students will start working earlier fostered by these partnerships and dropping out will decline.

❏ Internet shakeouts will increase as many dot.com companies fail; those that survive will be economic forces to contend with.

❏ All ages and diverse groups will be working elbow to elbow in organizations.

Generations in the Workplace

There is a widening difference in points of view, values, experience, expectations, frames of reference, communication skills, and abilities among different generations who now find themselves working together in organizations. How do you relate to individuals who have a different mindset from you? How do you manage those who are younger or older than you? The stigma of changing jobs and careers has been lifted; the layoffs and downsizing of the 1980s drove many unsuspecting employees back into the job search process. They had to reinvent themselves—find new careers, new employers, and new locations. Those who have gone through this employment upheaval will definitely have a different attitude toward their job than those who entered the workforce at a time of nearly full employment, with employers desperate to hire.

Another change is that people are working longer. Over 70 percent of the current workforce expects to work past age 65—the traditional retirement age. Many older workers are opting for part-time, consulting, or free-agent status; others continue to work full time. Telecommuting will attract still others in the information fields.

Another fact is that employers are willing to salvage employees. Some organizations have staff members that search online for employees' résumés. Counteroffers are made to head off an employee's resignation. Even employees in fast-paced, high-tech organizations are looking for different kinds of perks. Words such as *respect, appreciation, honesty,* and *communication* are being used as the Internet culture is driving the reemergence of values in some workplaces. Many high-tech firms are spotlighting the interpersonal aspects of the employer-employee relationship; will it spill over into other areas? An article in *Fortune* (June 24, 2000) profiles Generation Y; this millennial generation says it does not want to live or work the way we do—but can we work together?

Diversity Issues

In April 2000, *The New York Times* reported that the Immigration and Nationalization Service (INS) was turning a blind eye to illegal immigrants—on a temporary basis—to ease the employment shortage. H1-B visas (a classification of visas which allows persons coming from other countries to work in the United States) are being issued more easily. Employers are not totally supportive of this stopgap measure and are concerned about continued shortages of employees. Because so many jobs are available, standard summer jobs, long the staple of high school and college students, are being passed over. For instance, the lifeguard shortage got so serious during the summer of 2000 in the New York City area that former lifeguards were called back into service; insurance salespersons, brokers, and bankers were watching the waters on weekends.

Recent immigrants are not only found working in big cities but are also working throughout the United States. These new hires bring another element into the workplace. Diversity issues, based on cultural and societal differences, are more prevalent in organizations than ever before. Language, attire, and communication styles are widely divergent. How do you cope with diversity? What solutions can you bring to the organization? What tactics and management skills would you use to deal with a staff that speaks four different languages? How would you accommodate differing religious holidays and a wide variety of traditional mores? How would you mold such diverse people into a cohesive team?

Diversity Exercise

List below at least 15 types of differences that you can think of when considering the diverse characteristics of the people you live and work with. (Some suggested answers are shown at the bottom of the exercises.)

(We did the first three to get you started.)

1. Gender

2. Race

3. Place of birth

4. _____

5. _____

6. _____

7. _____

8. _____

9. _____

10. _____

11. _____

12. _____

13. _____

14. _____

15. _____

Suggestions: age, school attended, economic status, social status, height, weight, level of fitness, choice of foods (meat, dairy, vegetarian), wears glasses/contacts, smoker, piercing, tattoos (and attitude toward same), veteran, disabled, religion, choice of home, marital status, parental status, attitudes toward fur, technology, pets, politics, television, music, theater, and more!

How Do You Communicate?

Never have more people been able to "reach out and touch someone" as in this cellular age. Laptops, handheld personal digital assistants (PDAs), and cellular telephones are the norm, not the exception. Mastering and managing these diverse modes of communication is one more requisite to employment. Being able to write and speak well have never been more critical as information and knowledge are being exchanged at a rapid rate. It used to be asked of applicants *Are you computer literate?"* Now, applicants may be expected to be versed in multiple computer programs and different modes of communication.

More types and insistent communication modes require better management skills. How do you prioritize when your E-mail is announcing *"You've got mail,"* your beeper is pinging, and your cell phone vibrating—all while you have someone in your office with you and you have a videoconference scheduled in 20 minutes? Being able to think—to hold a thought and carry it through despite multiple interruptions—is a valuable asset.

How Do You Communicate?
Which is your favorite way to communicate with others?
Rank these from No. 1 most favorite to least.
_____telephone
_____fax
_____E-mail
_____videoconference
_____letters, memos
_____face-to-face
_____other: _____
Why did you choose No. 1? _____
_____
What was your reason for choosing your least favorite?_____
_____
How do you like to be communicated with? _____
Why? _____

How Do You Stay Informed?

What do you read daily?

What do you read weekly?

What do you read monthly?

What do you read occasionally?

How else do you remain informed? (Websites, television, radio, classes, seminars, workshops, associations)

   Medium:

   Programs:

   Websites:

What have you learned today?

Technology News

What new skills, experiences, devices, and technologies have you mastered? What are you learning now? Even if you personally do not use all the latest gadgets, how do you deal with those who do? How do you interact with those on the cutting edge of technology or those hopelessly behind the times? Are you aware of what is happening in the world that will change the way business is being transacted? Do you have an open mind, a curiosity about new developments?

Reaction to Changes in the Workplace

Which one of these descriptions fits you?

> *"Things were so much easier before _____. In the past we used to _____," or "Did you see the article about _____? I wonder when we will start doing _____," or "Some companies are using _____. How can we get started with it?"*

How do you deal with and manage change? Change may present overwhelming challenges to some and an increase in adrenaline to others. Are you an innovator? Do you initiate change? Do you sponsor or encourage those who do innovate? Are you basically skeptical of new methods and ways of doing things? There is one certainty in the workplace today—things will change. Either due to competition, market conditions, technology, or management—tomorrow's organization will be different from today's.

Does change cause you concern?

"Will I be able to learn this new method?"

"Will I be able to perform as well?"

"How can I learn all these new requirements by next week?"

"What was wrong with the old way?"

How adaptable, flexible are you? Can you keep an open mind and be neutral in evaluating new techniques? How do you help others adapt?

New Job Issues

Flextime and job sharing were news years ago; now they are accepted in many organizations as a matter of course. Whether you accept a position because an organization offers flextime or job sharing or because you have the opportunity to work with others who participate in such programs, possibly even supervise them, how prepared are you?

With fast Internet and intranet connections, many employees now work full- or part-time at home as telecommuters. Is this something that you would consider? Would you be willing to work in the office 3 days and from out of your home for 2 days?

How would you supervise employees who are physically not on site? What problems and policies can you foresee? How would you expect to be managed by a supervisor if you worked at home? Are you proficient with required technology to share documents and files with others on an intranet?

Telecommuting Issues

Are you considering working from home? If you have never done this before, how do you know you will like it? If you are used to working in an office, the isolation and the feeling of being out of touch can be overwhelming. Being without the social aspects of going to work—the getting dressed, traveling, the camaraderie with coworkers, the stopping off for a bite to eat after work, the gossip—can be devastating to some workers and hardly noticed by others. Would you be happy going from bumping into coworkers on the way to the file cabinet to seeing no one? Do you share your living quarters with family, friends, or pets? How will they react? Can you work independently?

Do you have the space to devote to a home office? What about your family and neighbors: Once you are home and available, will you become the door-answerer and package-receiver? In addition to the space, do you have the wiring necessary?

Telecommuting Issues

- ❏ Does the organization have a telecommuter policy?
- ❏ If so, how long has this telecommuter policy been in effect?
- ❏ How many employees are telecommuters? What are their jobs? How many other telecommuters are under the same manager as me?
- ❏ How does the manager communicate with them?
- ❏ What equipment will be issued? What furniture will I be given?
- ❏ Is there a written job description? Are there written performance expectations?
- ❏ Will someone from the organization inspect the location to provide assistance in ensuring that the work environment is a safe and healthy one?
- ❏ What are the organization's requirements regarding this work space? What are the requirements for the care of the equipment I'm assigned?
- ❏ Will there be any inspections? If "yes," will they be announced? What will be their purpose?
- ❏ What are the organization's requirements regarding computer information security?
- ❏ What are the phone contact procedures?
- ❏ Is there a written telecommuter's agreement to sign?
- ❏ Will the organization install a separate telephone line? Computer data line? Fax line? Will it give a payment for rental of the space?
- ❏ Are there written guidelines for reporting a work-related accident?

Will you be faced with managing or having telecommuters as coworkers? Does the organization have a telecommuting policy? Are workers required to report to the office regularly? How will you ensure that the telecommuter feels included, knows about new developments at the office both business and social (retirements, birthday celebrations, new hires)? How can you help a worker in the transition to becoming a telecommuter? What about the telecommuters' peers who feel that working from home is a perk and are envious? How will you keep the team atmosphere amicable?

Below are issues you should address before committing yourself to telecommuting.

Telecommuter's Checklist

Before you plan to telecommute. ask yourself

❑ Is there adequate workspace for my current needs?

❑ Are there opportunities for future expansion?

❑ Do I have sufficient storage space?

❑ Do I have adequate and appropriate lighting?

❑ Is there sufficient ventilation and climate control?

❑ Are there a safe number of electrical circuits?

❑ Is it quiet enough for my concentration?

❑ Does the space allow for appropriate separation from home and family distractions?

❑ Is the space pleasant and comfortable?

❑ Is it close enough to needed business services?

❑ Are there any zoning or lease restrictions that preclude my telecommuting?

❑ Is there adequate insurance coverage (by the business) to protect the business equipment?

Outsourcing

If an organization is eliminating one or more functions because the function is not part of the core business and arranges to have the function performed by an outside vendor, that is called *outsourcing*. Sometimes the vendor will hire the employees who are currently working for the employer directly. This is done as a cost-saving measure—the vendor may sometimes use nonunion labor, and it reduces costs by lowering wages or benefits or both. Outsourcing represents one more opportunity for you to consider as a job prospect.

Contract or Freelance Work—the New Hired Hand

As organizations attempt not to repeat the errors of the past, one approach they take to help avoid the problem of bloating the size of the staff is to hire "accordion style" to fit the current needs of the organization. When more workers are needed to meet increasing or unique business demands, the organization will hire on a contract basis or from a freelance pool (that is, people who make themselves available on a project or short-term basis) and pay them as independent contractors on a "1099" (and not on a W-2 which is a federal form used solely to place a person on the employee payroll).

With such hires, the employer wins because it keeps payroll expenses down (no payroll taxes and no benefits), and frequently the people retained like it as well because they are in business for themselves. Keep in mind that in this arrangement you are not eligible for unemployment insurance when the assignment ends. Also if you are hurt while performing services for the organization, you are not eligible for unemployment compensation through the organization because you are not an employee. In the outsourced situation you are eligible for both since you are an employee of the organization who has employed you to provide service to the organization with whom they have the contract.

Case Study Questions

These are popular in some business circles and require the job candidate to solve a hypothetical business problem, on the spot. The types of questions are geared to the technical or managerial skills required for the position. There is no way to prepare specifically for these types of questions as they usually require a certain amount of subject matter expertise. The interviewer is looking to test your communication and analytical skills; find out if you are resourceful and creative; and determine how well you perform under pressure.

The format is that you are presented with a problem. You then probe for additional information, determining what additional information is needed and what inferences you can make from your knowledge base before coming up with a solution. There are usually several right answers, and how you arrive at them counts as much as the answer itself.

Questions

5.1 *Are you a shareholder?*

If you are, say so. Make a brief comment about why you decided to invest and keep your money in XYZ Company. Then be quiet. If your comment has made the interviewer angry, she or he may let you know right after your comment. If you do not own stock in the company, you could say *"Not yet but I want to because _____."* To say no and leave the statement stand on its own with no explanation is weak. Even *"I can't because I'm responsible for child support payments,"* is better, but you may get some hostile feelings from your comments.

5.2 *As a manager, how have you promoted diversity in the workplace?*

One unit under my leadership only had _____. I always feel that such a situation is never healthy so I worked with the supervisors reporting to me and sold them on the idea of making changes. Then I began to move individuals from the group to other units."

Another approach is

Whenever we had an opening, I asked HR to help correct past imbalances. I suggested that they should help us to find us a good employee for that position but try to find _____.

A variation of this question is: Describe the most diverse organization you ever worked for. Here again the result will be disclosure of the nature and range of the diversity.

5.3 *At your last job, how much of your work was done independently and how much was done as part of a team?*

This question may be raised in an effort to determine in what setting are you most effective. Prior to the interview, prepare a list of activities that you performed alone and a list of those you did in concert with others. Before the interview, calculate the percentages and make sure the two lists combine to total 100 percent.

I did approximately 75 percent of my work on my own. Weekly planning sessions and consultations with team members made up the other 25 percent.

5.4 Can you describe the organization's culture?

You need to. What you identify will give the interviewer a clue regarding your understanding of the culture. Start by determining if it is a strong or weak culture. (By the way, strong cultures are usually found in very successful organizations, and weak cultures are more likely to be in organizations that are also-rans. For further study, consult *Corporate Cultures, the Rites and Rituals of Corporate Life* by Terrence E. Deal and Allan A. Kennedy, Addison-Wesley, Reading, Massachusetts, 1982. Out only since 1982, it is already a classic.) Next indicate what makes the culture what it is.

Meetings always start on time.

The organization can't do enough for its employees. We get turkeys at Thanksgiving and bonuses for New Year's—and we still have a traditional pension plan along with summer Fridays where employees can go home at 1:00 P.M. if their workload permits.

5.5 Can you work with people with big egos or with fragile egos?

Say no, and this interview is over. The reason the question is being raised is because the company has a problem. Refrain from answering whether you like dealing with those folks—that wasn't the question asked—but make a point of demonstrating one or at most two situations that make for brief interesting stories to show that you can deal with ego problems effectively. Most importantly, close by asking, "Is that a problem here?" Then be quiet and listen very carefully to the answer.

5.6 Do you expect your current employer to make a counteroffer if you tender your resignation? Would you consider it?

If you say yes, you are portraying yourself as a highly regarded employee. If you say no without qualifying it—*"It's their policy to never give a counteroffer"*—you are denigrating yourself.

I would feel flattered that my current employer values me such that it would extend a counteroffer. But as you and I have discussed, the main reason I wanted to meet with your organization is because the opportunity is such a great one. I would certainly give my employer the courtesy and listen to what it has to say, but I would gracefully decline because the opportunity offered to me here is something it just cannot match.

5.7 Do you have voice mail?

An easy answer is no, but the questions below can still be raised in a hypothetical context, so be ready anyway. Find out if the interviewer's interest is primarily work, home, or both. Beware when responding that a negative answer may be interpreted as out-of-date and not "technically savvy."

5.8 What does your message say?

Here you have the opportunity to perform or keep it simple. We suggest the latter. If you are answering about your home phone, a response may be: *"Hi. You have just reached 617-555-1881. We are unable to take your call, but leave a message and we will return your call as soon as we can."* This is a professional statement, yet indicates a concern for privacy. Take the opportunity while reading this book to consider an answering machine—or if you already have one, consider the professionalism of your message.

5.9 How often do you change your message?

You may wonder why the interviewer is keeping this line of questioning going and where will it end. There may be a job-related concern because you are meeting with an organization that takes its voice messages seriously and expects them to always inform in a current accurate manner.

Whenever I am away from the office for more than 2 hours, I direct my calls to my assistant.

5.10 How often do you check for messages?

Usually once every 2 hours, but if there is a particular call I'm waiting for, I direct callers to contact me on my cell phone.

5.11 If you had reached my voice mail, what message would you have left?

"Hello, this is (your full name). I am calling at the suggestion of (insert the name of the person who referred you here). Please call me at your earliest convenience. I will be available from 2 to 4 this afternoon. My number is _____. Thank you. I look forward to your call."

5.12   *Do you need everyone to like you?*

These are still touchy-feely times, so do not be surprised to hear such a question. The big point here is that you are not being hired by vote or as a result of a popularity contest. You are being hired to do a job and that includes all aspects of the job—whether the elements of the job make you popular or not. At the same time, be careful not to come across as a total-ly task-oriented person. Make the point that compassion is important and that you have a respect for others that is not to be ignored. The main point you are trying to make is that you need to rely on your staff for key ac-complishments, but if any members of the staff stand in the way, they need to be dealt with regardless of whether they like you for it or not.

5.13   *Do you see your current or former coworkers socially?*

How times have changed. Not too long ago this question would not have mattered, but now your affirmative answer is an indication that you are a team player—a real positive point for a job seeker of any age but espe-cially important if you are over 50 because you are demonstrating you see the importance of belonging.

> *We had a practice of volunteering in a reading program at a local school which I still continue. Often, a group of us from my old department will meet to cel-ebrate a birthday or promotion.*

5.14   *Do you think that honesty is always the best policy?*

How could you answer anything but a direct affirmative here? To be on the safe side, you might only add one caveat—you don't have to be *too* honest. For instance, if an employee wears an outlandish outfit on casual Friday, you do not need to go out of your way to say what you really think of the outfit. On the other hand, you may take the posture that honesty and credibility go hand in hand, even if this means telling the boss some-thing he or she doesn't want to hear. Of course whether the boss really wants to hear the truth once you are hired is another matter, but just about all think they want the truth and that they don't want yes people around them. By the way, honesty keeps things simple because you don't have to remember who you told what to whom.

5.15   *Do you think loyalty will return to the workplace?*

> *Loyalty needs to be a reciprocal process that builds over time as the relation-ship between the employee and the employer grows.*

Then ask, *"What do you think?"* This will give you a chance to get some insight into the person sitting across from you.

5.16 How do you build relationships with new customers?

I start by showing new customers what a good listener I am. (I like to believe that is how I got them to be a customer in the first place—by determining who they are and what is important to them.) While I'm listening, I'm constantly asking myself what can I do to help them fill their needs. In addition to the business side, there is also the soft side. Who is this person in front of me? I look around the office and see what the person has around him or her—pictures of the family or boats, for instance. There may be a leftover balloon from a birthday celebration, a Yankees cap, and a school mug. All these items tell you something about what is important to this person who is your customer. I become a sponge and try to absorb it all. Then I make notes and put them in my organizer. When I make the next contact, I will raise one, two, or three comments on the personal side. Meanwhile I am always making sure that she or he is quite happy with our products and services. I look for opportunities to sell other items we have that will make his or her life easier and more effective.

5.17 How do you cope with pressure?

I thrive under pressure.

Too much pressure is not a good thing, but some pressure and a sense of urgency is helpful in getting tasks accomplished and hitting targets.

If the pressure becomes too great, I take a step back and review my priorities and make sure that nothing is falling through the cracks. If the situation starts to become overwhelming, I make sure that I personally brief my manager. I include alternative action plans in the discussion that I suggest as solutions.

Have an example ready in case one would help you show your effectiveness in pressure-filled situations. Make it brief and to the point, and be sure that you present the story coherently and in measured tones.

5.18 How do you resolve diversity problems?

This question is a triple zinger. The interviewer is putting you on the spot by making you say (1) I recognize diversity as an important issue, (2) you have experienced problems in your organization's attempts to be diverse, and (3) this is what diversity means to you.

I always try to keep it simple. First I define the diversity problem. For example, we do not have enough minorities and women among our management trainees. Then I do a gap analysis, measuring the size of the gap between where we are (current staff profile) and where we should be (desired target profile). First I determine how many minorities and women we have at the

present time. Then I estimate how many we need in order to be considered di-
verse. Last I set out to identify, with a staff brainstorming session, various
action alternatives with goals and timetables that would provide us with
opportunities to close the gap. How do you do it here?

5.19   How would you deal with a frustrated or unhappy employee?

I would meet with the employee privately in an attempt to first let the em-
ployee know my concern and second to try to get the employee to discuss the
frustration or the cause of the unhappiness with me. I would tell him or her
the purpose of the meeting and then be quiet. That should be a real opportu-
nity for the employee to open up. If he or she doesn't, I would not grow frus-
trated and or take it personally.

5.20   Is how you say something as important as what you say? Or more important?

More than ever before we need to be careful about how we say something
whenever we communicate in the workplace. If sufficient attention is not paid
to the "how," the "what" may easily be lost. I was with a company that was
not doing very well. It could afford only a 2 percent increase in budgeted pay-
roll. The organization had always paid careful attention to internal commu-
nication. When senior management asked that the word about raises be passed
down the line, employees were not surprised and in fact were pleased that the
organization had found a way to give anything at all. Down the street, a
company going through better days had to face a workforce that was disap-
pointed with an 8 percent budget increase for raises.

With growing diversity in the workplace, clear communication is
increasingly important. The filters through which individuals process
messages are varied. Third World countries (one of which may be an employee's place of origin) are now just an air flight away. Also that person
may be a graduate of the Harvard Business School as well. Additionally,
there are always gender communication differences and age differences
to add more layers of filters that process every message. This information
should be part of your preparation for answering this question.

5.21   Our vision is to be different from and better than any other (retail/telecom/entertainment/E-commerce) company. What does this mean to you?

This represents an open invitation to join the bandwagon for industry
leadership. The interviewer wants to determine whether you have the
passion the organization is looking for.

That is a big reason why I am meeting with you today. I like everything I hear and read and see about this company. It is striving for excellence in everything it wants to do. I want to be a part of the staff that gets it there and then sustains those excellent qualities that put it at the top of its class.

5.22 What do you think the key is to good communication?

Listening is always the key. The essential part of listening is the opportunity to get feedback. With everybody being barraged with messages from advertisers and everyone else, we are all competing for the attention of the person we are trying to give a message to. Only if I am sure the person really received and understood my message can I be certain that I communicated effectively.

5.23 We will call you in 6 to 8 weeks—we make these decisions very carefully.

We are including this because the interviewer is asking for buy-in and he or she will take silence or no comment as your agreement. If you wish, you may ask in response, *"Is this code for 'we are not interested in you'?"* The fact is that this may not be the case at all. In the current environment there is turbulence and a lot of unusual comments—like this one—so don't take it personally and don't be surprised. If you have the notion, you may ask *"How will the organization perform with this position vacant for that period of time?"* If you haven't been told already, this may also be the time to ask if this is a new position. The reason for the time lag may also be due to the anticipated generation of business or the start of a commitment that is now "in the works." Regardless of the reasoning, the more information you are able to obtain here, the more insight you will get into the decision-making process of the organization.

5.24 What are your location preferences?

This question has always been asked, but in the past it was done to establish that the organization is in charge. You would be asked and then assigned a location. If the assignment differed from your choice and you refused it, you would likely be a marked person. Now there is less likelihood that you would have problems if you refused to relocate. Nowadays if an organization could not give you your desired location, it would most likely offer you incentives. The point here is that if you have a preference for a location, you would be foolish to say something like, *"It really doesn't matter."* If you are unsure, say, *"I would like to consider each of the sites and then get back to you. Is the end of the week okay?"* Then do research to determine which location appears to be the best from an organizational and career standpoint. Whenever you are given choices, do not squander them but make decisions based on research. No one is more interested in your career than you.

5.25 *What are your primary activities outside of work?*

Don't say something shocking here. If the question is asked, try to identify a few activities that you enjoy doing that are likely to be shared by your interviewer. If you see model sailboats and seascapes all over the office, you may assume the person you are dealing with is a sea lover. Watch out though that you have a genuine knowledge and appreciation for whatever you are selecting for two reasons: The interviewer may come back with, "Actually this isn't my office," or question you on the subject of boats to determine whether you have a sincere interest or just a shallow appreciation of questionable intent.

5.26 *What are your priorities?*

In the old days, no one had to ask this question because everyone, it seemed, shared the same priorities—family, country, and religion. Duties toward these three things meant working for a living as a means to an end. Now our diverse working population has a wide range of priorities sometimes starting with "me" and covering just about everything else. There is no guarantee that work is considered the means to an end. In the interview, keep your response simple and compatible if possible with those you imagine may be the priorities of the person interviewing you. Some organizations love to hear *"I live to work"* while others frown on this. Be prepared and speak briefly about what is important to you.

> *In addition to providing a livelihood, I would like to be fortunate to have a job in a career that is truly exciting to me.*

5.27 *What constructive criticism have you received from employers?*

Remember you are not on the psychologist's couch. With any question that seeks a self-indictment (Too strong a term? The answer could in fact have that effect), you need to be careful that you identify strengths that others may have mislabeled.

> *One thing that has been pointed out to me is that I stay too long at work— that I should be careful of burnout. While it is certainly true that I probably spend about 60 hours a week at work (and I take some home besides), I always ask if I don't do the work who will?*

Or

I have been told on occasion that I have been too client/customer-focused. My answer always is 'I don't understand. Can you ever be too client/customer-focused?'

5.28 What criteria are you using to evaluate organizations?

Choose any or all of the ones below and you can't go wrong.

There are several criteria that I consider. The first is the business the organization is in. I really need to consider those organizations that produce something that I can be proud of and have a passionate feeling for. Second what is management like? Third how do they treat their people? Fourth how sound are they financially? Fifth what kind of career prospects will I have there? And sixth will I be secure financially?

5.29 What do you expect to experience in this job that you did not experience in your last job?

An astute question if there ever was one. The key here is to either describe a situation that either compares to or contrasts with the interviewing organization. Point out what the potential employer has that is positive (such as great market position or growing product line) or does not have (such as high turnover in management, problems with suppliers) that is another positive aspect.

In my last job, they said that my position was such a priority that they would provide whatever resources I needed to help me to make the position an effective one. After my arrival, I found several other recent hires had been told the same thing. What we were all required to do was compete for the limited resources the organization was willing to provide.

Or

At _____ company, my supervisor was extremely hands-on. I am not saying that there is anything wrong with that. It is just that I do not need that kind of micromanagement. Here, from your style, it seems that you welcome my "low maintenance" approach.

6
Self-Assessment

To assess yourself, start with what you know. You know yourself—or at least you think you do. There are three of you involved in the job search process:

Who you are.

Who you think you are.

Who others think you are.

Then there are all the roles that you play: Daughter, son, mother, father, uncle, aunt, friend, neighbor, supervisor, coworker, student. Who are you today? Who are you now? Who is going on the interview?

You know what you like, what you do best, what motivates you, what turns you off, but can you convey these characteristics in an interview? Furthermore, are you selling the right you to the right employer?

Much of the job search is marketing. In order to make a sale, you first have to understand the particulars of the product (which is you). What is it you are supposed to do for the organization? What needs can you satisfy? Then, an understanding of the consumers' (that is, the employers') needs is essential. What are their problems? What solutions are sought? Why you can satisfy their needs better, faster, cheaper . . . .

Before your sales pitch can go forward, the product—you—must be thoroughly investigated. Each time you target an organization and a job opening, you should review the reasons why you should be hired. You will find these reasons in your self-assessment.

Even Superman was a master at self-assessment and the art of marketing himself. He knew his weaknesses: Lois Lane and Kryptonite! He had reduced his sales pitch to, *"More powerful than a locomotive, faster than a speeding bullet, able to leap tall buildings in a single bound."* He knew what to sell about himself.

Relevant Skills, Experience, Qualities, Talents, Gifts, Interests

The key word is *relevant*. The ability to leap tall buildings in a single bound may be impressive but, unless the organization needs such an astounding skill, it is quite extraneous to your job candidacy. The key to successful self-assessment is a two-step process:

1. Discovering and understanding the skills you have to offer.
2. Discovering and understanding the skills needed and wanted by the organization.

This *matching* of skills to needs is essential to target the job and the organization. Also it is essential in successful interviewing. It is a case of *"You need . . ."* and *"I can provide . . . ."*

Discovering Your Skills

First do not limit your consideration to only those activities that are work-related. Expand your consideration to all areas of your life—leisure, academic, community service, and private. Second do not limit yourself to verbs—that is, those action words you used in your résumé and marketing letter. Expand your thinking to adjectives and nouns.

For example, if you are a student, you may not have credited yourself with your skills in time management and organizing. Learning how to research organizations online during your job search is another skill that you should not overlook. Planning, memorizing, negotiating—these are skills you may have been born with or have acquired along the way. These are your "verb" skills that describe the *what you can do*.

Then, there are all the *things you know* how to use and subjects you have some expertise in. Fashion, computers, bicycles, the Japanese language, and digital cameras are all subject matters that you may have knowledge of.

Last there are all the *qualities* that describe you. Calm, incisive, procrastinating, creative, dependable, and eclectic can be used to describe someone. Which words would you use to describe you?

Make a list for each of these categories and cite an example as proof that you have the skill, knowledge, or quality. An example of proof might be: *"I am* supportive *because I have worked and contributed to team efforts both at my job at ABC Company and in my leisure time spent as a member of a rowing team. This is how I prefer to work and how I do my best—as part of a team."*

What I Can Do	
List those skills that are verbs—what you can do. Next to each, list an example of your use of this skill.	
Skill	**Proof**

What I Know	
List what you know—subjects and areas of your expertise. Include an example of this knowledge in the Proof column.	
Knowledge	**Proof**

This Is What I Am Like

List the adjectives that describe your qualities. Provide an example for each in the Proof column.

Qualities	Proof

Writing Your History

If you have not completed a detailed review of your employment, write your employment history now. This information will be helpful to you in reviewing your experience to date as well as providing details for job applications. Even though you may choose what to highlight in your résumé or discuss in an interview, include all your experiences; do not neglect short-term positions, temporary assignments, or internships. These might provide sources of valuable skills or experiences that you may have forgotten.

To write your education history, first consider whether you have graduated within the past 5 years or have taken any classes. Regardless of your graduation date, do not overlook any seminars or workshops you attended while you were on the job or elsewhere.

Weaknesses in Skills, Experience, Education, and Employment

We cannot be all things to all employers, and there is no one perfect hire for each position. However, there can be a best candidate. You have to be their best choice. We all have ways to compensate for our shortcomings. Those who tend to forget details become note-takers. If planning is your weak suit, have you taken to getting to work early to make a "to do" list? We invent our own ways to get the job done with all our imperfections intact. Everyone who hated to do business on the telephone applauded the advent of E-mail and became superb in the art of concise, well-written cybermemos. Recognizing your shortcomings gives you an opportunity to deal with them in advance of an interview. Someone observed that experts don't not make mistakes, they just don't repeat them!

Unique Skills

You realize that many of your skills and much of your expertise can be used by different organizations and in different types of jobs. Other skills may be specific to only one organization, such as a particular software package that was created specifically for use in one organization. However, your ability to learn and understand a program is a transferable skill. It is this category of transferable skills that are highly desired and can only be sold to others if you recognize them in your professional and educational histories.

Professional History

List the last five jobs or jobs you held over the past 15 years. If there was only one employer, list former employers. Start with current or last employer.

Date(s): _____ to _____

Employer: _____

Location: _____ Supervisor: _____

Most recent/last position: _____

Starting position: _____

Starting salary: _____ Ending/recent salary: _____

Job title: _____

Job description: _____

* * * * * *

Date(s): _____ to _____

Employer: _____

Location: _____ Supervisor: _____

Most recent/last position: _____

Starting position: _____

Starting salary: _____ Ending/recent salary: _____

Job title: _____

Job description: _____

* * * * * *

Date(s): _____ to _____

Employer: _____

Location: _____ Supervisor: _____

Most recent/last position: _____

Starting position: _____

Starting salary: _____ Ending/recent salary: _____

Job title: _____

Job description: _____

* * * * * *

Education History

List most recent first. Include all workshops, seminars, and classes taken.

Date(s): _____ to _____

School/Institution: _____

Location: _____

Course of study/title of course: _____

_____

Degree/certificate: _____

* * * * * *

Date(s): _____ to _____

School/Institution: _____

Location: _____

Course of study/title of course: _____

_____

Degree/certificate: _____

* * * * * *

Date(s): _____ to _____

School/Institution: _____

Location: _____

Course of study/title of course: _____

_____

Degree/certificate: _____

* * * * * *

Stress the Positives

Be honest. What are your weaknesses? Hate to speak in public? Do you take extra time to plan and practice and just get up and do it anyways? Or do you have the knack of finding someone who loves doing it and is great too? That is a positive way of dealing with a shortcoming. What about those skills or qualities required by the organization or job for which you do not have a match? What do you have to offer instead to get the job done?

Matching

Listing what you have to offer is only half of the challenge. You must now consider what the market wants. What do the organization(s) and job opening(s) that you have targeted require? This step requires research and analysis on your part: two more skills!

First, describe the *organization*. Is it a new, middle-aged, or mature organization? Each has particular needs. What are its products and services, and how does it do business? What is the management style? Is it team-

Target Organization
Name:
Location(s):
Main office:
Started:
Industry:
Products/services:
Markets:
Competitors:
Website:
E-commerce:
Management:
Culture:
Current events/problems:

based? What is the culture of the organization? What are the current problems the organization is facing? Where have you worked that is similar in
size, scope, or management style?

Second, look at the *job opening* you are targeting. What are the key requirements, responsibilities, and demands of the job? What skills and
qualities are needed for the position? The skills needed for an art ap-
praiser are different from those of an air-traffic controller. What type and
range of skills are needed for your targeted job?

Now do the matching. This in essence is your sales pitch; your answer
to why they should hire you! Make your list of "Organization needs" and
"I can provide," choosing at least five major needs. Making this list is possible only after you have researched the targeted organization and job
opening and have looked at yourself and your skills critically. If you have
done detailed employment and education histories as part of your preparation for writing a résumé, refer to them. If they are not current (or you
have not done so), you can take the opportunity to do so now.

Target Job Opening
Organization:
Location(s):
Job title (description):
Corporate title:
Department/division:
Report to:
Prime responsibilities:
Skills needed:
Technical requirements:
Personal qualities needed:

Matching Exercise
Organization:
Job: Date:

1. Organization needs:
 	
    Why?
 	
  I can provide:

2. Organization needs:
 	
    Why?
 	
  I can provide:

3. Organization needs:
 	
    Why?
 	
  I can provide:

4. Organization needs:
 	
    Why?
 	
  I can provide:

5. Organization needs:
 	
    Why?
 	
  I can provide:

6. Organization needs:
 	
    Why?
 	
  I can provide:

What Can You Do to Improve Yourself during the Job Search?

When was the last time you took a class in your field? Do you belong to any professional organizations? What is on your reading list? How do you keep up to date professionally? What are the trends in your industry? What skills have you acquired lately? If ads for jobs for which you wish you could apply list requirements that you do not have, what are you doing now to change that situation? What are your long-range plans? What are you doing now to get yourself there?

It Is More than an Interview

Your self-assessment is simply not idle thoughts although many of what you've listed will be raised in interviews. Even if you get through an interview without them surfacing, you should have answers for yourself. Knowing that you have specific skills and experiences that can be valued by an employer will boost your confidence enormously before and during the interview. The fact that you have considered the organization's needs and the job's requirements and matched them to what you can offer will prepare you for the hard questions asked in the interview (*"Why should we hire you?"* for example).

Additionally it is easy to claim, *"I can do that!"* but it is much more meaningful to relate a short example of when you have actually done it! Having an arsenal of anecdotes to illustrate a variety of your skills and experiences, particularly when faced with the *"What would you do if . . . ?"* or *"Tell me about a time when . . . ."* questions can help you immensely during an interview. These accomplishments and achievements are your claims to the job itself.

Interview Tactics

There are endless variations to tactics in an interview. Questions can range from general to specific subject matter expertise. For example, you may be asked to discuss a time when you:

❏ Turned down a good job.

❏ Had to fire a friend.

❏ Were disappointed in your performance.

❏ Were tolerant of an opinion different from yours.

Professional To Do List	
These are areas that I recognize that I must improve or skills/experience I must acquire and my plans on how I will do so.	
To Do:	**My Plan:**

❑ Handled a difficult situation with a coworker.

❑ Had to make an unpopular decision.

❑ Missed a deadline.

❑ Made a poor decision.

❑ Made a good decision with incomplete information.

❑ Used creative means to solve a problem.

❑ Persuaded team members to accept your proposal.

❑ Enabled a program to be accepted by using political means.

❑ Created a strategy for completing a complex project.

❑ . . . etc.

These kinds of questions are the reason you completed a self-assessment as well as looked for ways to prove your skill level and experience. You need a repertoire of short stories or anecdotes to pepper your narra-

Recent Activities
What are you doing for yourself personally and professionally to improve your skills, acquire experience, or learn new ways of doing things?
1.
2.
3.
4.
5.

tives with. An interviewer may not remember all the details, but he or she will remember a good story! Have examples ready—none longer than 1 minute. Here's a sample: *"The most difficult task I recently had was to create a brochure practically overnight. The manager neglected to give me the disk with the template, so I had to do it from scratch. Second, the artwork to be inserted was nowhere to be found. I went through prior publications and inserted samples which I scanned in. Last, I got a small team together to write and proofread the copy. Ten hours later, it was done."*

Long-range Goals
Write down where you would like to see yourself in 10 years. Next, list the steps or actions that you should take to accomplish this goal.

10 year GOAL:

_____

_____

Why is this your goal? _____

❑ Step:

❑ Step:

❑ Step:

❑ Step:

❑ Step:

❑ Step:

❑ Step:

❑ Step:

Accomplishments

List your accomplishments; quantify when possible and relate each to the targeted organization and job opening.

Accomplishment Results, actions taken, problem faced	Details Where, when, how much	How Related?
1		
2		
3		
4		

Questions

6.1   Describe a situation where you found yourself differing from others on how to achieve a goal. Why did you differ? What actions did you take? What was the result?

When the company got a notification for nonpayment of payroll taxes from the IRS, I was expected to provide an explanation, even though I became an employee after the event took place. Although I had responsibility for payroll, accounting was responsible for paying the taxes. Yet they were not being held accountable for this nonpayment. I promised this would never happen again, so I shopped the payroll with a vendor that would take responsibility for tax payments. When I found a reliable vendor and a reasonable price, I asked several key members of management to attend the vendor's presentation. I met separately with members of the accounting department. When they shared with me their very positive opinion regarding my suggestion, I knew the proposal would be accepted and it was. Needless to say I never got another IRS notification.

Other questions can concentrate on subject matter expertise; this is very much related to the 'try before you buy' reasoning. Refer to the lists and proofs you made for things you know and things you can do. What possible expertise questions can you face?

❏ Why do you prefer Unix over other platforms?

❏ What do you feel is a good policy for dealing with _____?

❏ How did you feel about the recent ruling on copyright infringement?

❏ Do you prefer using a VB346X1 or a GT401x3, and why?

Even though it may not be as popular as other programs, I have used MSPublisher for years and have always been impressed with its easy-to-use toolbars as well as its sophisticated menu layout. The ability to quickly E-mail mockups has made the proofing easier, too.

6.2   Have you ever offered suggestions to members of management? How did they respond?

The organization allowed a part-time facilities manager to charge the organization for any construction work given to his contracting company. I suggested that the organization was losing two ways. First, because the demands of the facility were such that a full-time facilities manager was needed. And second, when any contracting work was done, the part-time employee would obviously be biased by the work his own firm could do and so the organization suffered from lost opportunities for competitive bidding and a lack of distribution of work. I brought this to the attention of my manager who moved it up the line. Three months later we hired a full-time facilities manager who did not moonlight by running his own firm. No one ever called to say great idea, but I had personal satisfaction from realizing that I helped to make the organization run more effectively in both the short run and long run.

6.3 Describe an ideal work team.

It takes a shared mission. There are all types of people with many different skills. Communication is essential to determine what will be done, when it will be done, and by whom. This "buying in" to the project can occur only when each team member understands the mission, the purpose of the project, and the vision of the outcome.

6.4 How did your job description change for your last job while you were in it?

I have a tendency to make any job I am in expand the more I am in it. That was especially true in my last job. When I got there, the position was limited to processing paperwork from the field, reviewing it, and making it presentable for the centralized accounting department. If anything was out of order, it would be sent back for correction. The more I was in the job, the more I realized that if I could identify the problem (missing items, supporting documentation) and add what was missing, the more quickly the form would be processed. I suggested this to my boss, and she bought into it. Then she suggested I rewrite the procedure and once that was done, I was asked to rewrite the procedures when we went to a six sigma approach.

6.5 Describe your personality.

Again remember your audience, and do not under any circumstances describe your dysfunctional qualities, even in jest. Highlight briefly those aspects of your personality that will be most relevant on the job and at the same time convey a bias toward action.

I feel I am a generous person who is very much based in reality; quick to make friends and delighted to be a part of a team-building process. Life really excites me, and I see each day as an opportunity to grow personally and professionally. At the end of the day I easily go to sleep reviewing the accomplishments of the past day and feeling exhilarated with the thoughts of what is to be done tomorrow.

6.6 What personal quality makes you the perfect hire for this position?

For me it would be integrity. Doing the right thing, even if it is difficult, even when there is little time or a tight budget. When I do the right thing, I'm living up to the commitment I made when I was hired.

6.7   If you could change one aspect of your personality, what would it be?

The goal here is to do two things. First, be sure not to admit to any personality flaws. Second, identify a personality trait that is in fact positive if viewed the right way.

There isn't one aspect I would change but rather modify. It is my bias for action. Occasionally, this approach encourages action at a time when a slight delay might, in fact, be more appropriate. I should concentrate more on waiting until I have sufficient information—without dragging a situation—and then act instead of sometimes acting on incomplete information.

Or

I take my work very seriously and do not appreciate people who don't. Especially in this diverse environment, I need to realize that not everyone is as passionate about his or her work as I am.

6.8   What values are important to you?

Excellence and effectiveness are two values that really matter to me. If you are going to do anything at all, I really believe you need to do the absolute best you can. Also, too many people think that success is tied to effort, and they think that they are entitled to be successful because they worked hard. Not true. It is what you do and how you do it that is more important than how much you do. Results are easier to measure than effort, so we should think and behave that way as well.

6.9   Which of your skills do you feel needs to be developed more? What are you plans to do so?

Through my past jobs I have learned a lot about the paper industry. I also follow the trade journals. However, my knowledge of inks has been limited to the printing industry; a working knowledge of other media used for paper products would be an asset. I have recently joined the Paper Products Association to learn more.

6.10   Tell me about a time when you had to work with an employee whose performance was not up to par. How did you handle it?

I pride myself on being observant and knowing my staff's strengths and weaknesses. My first reaction would be that there is some sort of problem—either personal or work-related—that is affecting performance. I would call the employee aside and would tell him or her what I had observed and wait for a re-

sponse. If a problem was brought to light, then we would work together to find solutions. In closing, I would ask to follow up in a week's time to discuss how the performance has changed since our talk.

6.11 Which skill do you think is essential to this job? Why?

It is definitely being organized. Organizing my daily to-do list for the next day before I leave work. Keeping my computer files arranged logically. Setting up a framework for each day, allowing time to make and return telephone calls, catch up on mail, visit department heads if necessary. My organizational skill extends to my staff, with regular meetings and reviews of project status.

7
Getting Ready
for the Interview

One aspect of the job search and interview process we have not stressed is the physical one. Too often physical exercise gets the short shrift. Do not let this happen to you. When you are running, riding a bike, exercising, or merely taking a walk, the change of pace (literally) is a salve for the entire body. Your mind takes a welcome break, and you may find yourself coming back to your job search with renewed vigor and determination. Also do not discount your subconscious—it may be problem-solving while you are exerting yourself physically. If you are not doing so now, add regular physical exercise to your job search schedule. You will feel more fit and less resentful of the entire process if you do something for yourself! Additionally, it can be a great stress reliever.

Do not discount the personal appearance factor. There is a dichotomy in America's psyche—fast food (or is it fast fat?) establishments and health clubs are often next door to each other. Employees working long hours and then sending out for pizza while at work has become a tradition in some professional areas. Sitting for long hours at a computer has replaced long hours of physical labor as employment for many. Even though it may not be politically correct to say so, many employers, if given a choice, would rather have healthy-looking, attractive staff members than those who are not. This does not mean that you must evoke fashion model standards, but presenting a clean, healthy, and professional appearance will impress many interviewers.

Even though content is of prime importance in preparing and conducting an effective interview, packaging does count. Do not wait until the last minute to choose what you will wear. Be certain it is clean, pressed, and does not need repair; it must suit the venue. Look as if you already work there—or a little better! If it is a very casual atmosphere, still dress up. Just because the employees wear beach sandals and jeans to the office, does not mean you should show up for an interview dressed that way.

Getting Started

There is only one kind of preparation for an interview—thorough preparation. No matter how many interviews you have been on, no matter the reason for this interview, and no matter how busy you are with other tasks, each interview deserves attention. Sometimes the only thing that separates you from the other candidates is that you actually know what the company does! Three steps is all it takes:

1. Research
2. Rehearse
3. Relax

Research

Start with what you know. *What do you want? What do you need?* The greater your knowledge of your own needs (both financial and personal) and the ideal workplace environment that you envision, the better you will be able to target organizations and jobs that will excite you (raising your enthusiasm for the interview itself) as well as match you to positions that you are well suited for.

Be pragmatic. The first level of inquiry should be financial because very few of us are in a position not to consider this a priority. You should have in mind a salary range that satisfies your financial needs and is realistic in the marketplace. Do not limit yourself to salary alone—there are other elements that are equally important, such as:

❏ *Commute:* A longer or more expensive commute will affect your cash needs; conversely, a shorter travel time could be a positive element.

❏ *Location:* Will you consider relocating or is this absolutely not an option? Are there areas near you that you would not consider working in?

❏ *Culture:* Will you have to buy a new wardrobe to "fit in"? Is eating at your desk the norm? Is the office located in an area surrounded by only expensive eating establishments? Will yours be the only car in the corporate parking lot older than 5 years? What appears to be the average age of employees? Do they participate in after-hours activities (bowling leagues, softball games, ski trips)?

❏ *Other compensation:* No longer viewed as frills, for some time cell
phones, PDAs, beepers, and laptops have been heavily used in many
organizations. Will they provide these items for you? Likewise, for the
company car. Will you get employee discounts at local stores and for
the company product? Are there other perks that you will qualify for?
(Ford Motor Company, in early 2000, offered a new computer to every
employee to use at home.)

❏ *Personal requirements:* What do you need in terms of health-care benefits, insurance, savings or retirement plans, as well as child-care and
family leave policies? Depending on your age and stage in life, these
issues can take on great importance. What are you willing to trade
away (find outside child-care options in exchange for a shorter commute, less time away from home)?

To focus on your situation, complete a Needs versus Wants worksheet.
You may want a salary of $150,000 but you are willing to start at $125,000.
Other items, such as health-care benefits, may not be negotiable. These
items can be part of your external research (What are the employee benefits at ABC Company?) or during later-stage interviews when an offer is
made. In any case, these are the questions that you feel must be answered
before you can accept any job and are essential to negotiating a job offer.

Marketing Plan

When you first targeted organizations and job openings, when you wrote
your résumé and marketing letter, and when you did the matching exercise in Chapter 6, you highlighted your key sales points. Now, focus on
those sales points more closely.

Why should they hire you? Before every job interview, list for yourself
three to four reasons why you are ideal for that particular position at that
specific organization. Next to each reason, cite the proof. For example, if
one of your reasons is, *"I can increase your production without increasing
costs,"* then, in the next column, give a specific example from your work
experience showing why this statement can be relied on. *"At ABC, Inc., I
changed the production schedule, allowing for flextime for the crew, and increased
output 8 percent without any increase in costs. In fact, overall costs went down
2 percent because of better employee morale and less downtime."* These mini-
scenarios are the base line for your interview—the questions that you
hope interviewers will ask (and if they do not, you will introduce into the
conversation.) *It is very important that these key points are targeted to your
audience*—the organization where you are interviewing—and should be
reviewed and changed for different organizations.

Needs versus Wants

List below all the elements you would consider for a new job. Determine what your parameters are—what you hope to get and what you can accept. Add your own. Then assign a priority number to each.

Considerations:	Want:	Need:	Priority No.
Salary			
Location			
Industry			
Position/title			
Size of organization			
Culture			
Benefits			

Why _____ Organization Should Hire Me for _____ (Position)	
Targeted Point: Key skills and experiences needed for the job	**Proof:** Include quantifiers (how many, how much, what size)

These are the same strong points you will come back to when you close the interview and ask for the job, if you want it. And these same points are referred to in the closing of your thank-you letter when, again, you ask for the job.

References

You know you will be asked to provide references, either as a typed list or on an application form. Do not release names and telephone numbers of your current employer until after you have been offered the position and you have accepted. Also, don't list references without first asking the people you plan to list. Whom will you ask? There are two categories of references: personal and professional.

Personal references. Choose people whom know you in a professional capacity, not your dentist or godmother. Consider choosing peers, colleagues, members of professional associations, and even former customers or suppliers.

Professional references. Other than your current employer, offer the names of past employers and supervisors. If you have given seminars or workshops, include those names as well. Recent graduates can include instructors from their major courses of study and extracurricular activities. Some typical questions asked of references are:

What is your relationship to the candidate?

How long did you work with or supervise this person?

What was his or her title?

What results was he or she required to produce?

Please rate the candidate on a scale of 1 to 10:

Overall job performance

Flexibility on the job

Completion of assignments with few guidelines

Ability to improve situations or solve problems

Ability to work with a team

Ability to meet deadlines

Ability to establish rapport with others

Ability to adjust to rapidly changing situations

Do you have any comments you would like to add?

As you prepare for your interviews, also prepare your list of references so that you can refer to it when you complete application forms. If you omit your current employer, you can provide the list to your interviewer if asked. As mentioned earlier, as a courtesy, you should always ask in advance the individuals you are listing as references if they are willing to provide a reference for you. Once you have provided their names and contact numbers, be certain to let them know that you have done so; providing them with basic information about the organization and the job opening will enable them to give a more informed and relevant reference for you. Another reason for contacting them before you list them is to ensure the contact information you provide is current.

External Research

An interviewer at a company in New Haven loved to perplex candidates with the simple question *"Which industry are we in?"* Reactions from the applicants ranged from the stammered, *"I am not quite sure"* to a confident, *"You are an Internet company"* (even though it had a dot.com-related name, it was in the telecommunication industry). This just underscores the lack of basic research done by many job seekers before an interview.

"What business are we in?" is a different question. Is the telecommunication company in sales, marketing, hardware development, or manufacturing?

How can you present yourself as a knowledgeable, qualified, and enthusiastic job candidate if you do not know the first thing about the organization that is interviewing you? If you cannot take the time to learn about the job, the organization, and the industry, why should the organization take the time to learn about you?

What should you know about an organization before an interview? Granted, even with the Internet, detailed information is not available on every organization—but there is some information out there about virtually every organization, and you should be able to find it without being a Sherlock Holmes. Start with the basic list (see below) and see what information is available. Then, during the interview, attempt to fill in the blanks as you see fit. Certainly, it is not essential to know the exact date that a company was founded or by whom, but it is important to know if this is a 100-year-old, 10-year-old or 6-month-old, publicly held or family-owned company. Is this a technology-savvy organization? Does it have a Website? Is the site for promotional or sales purposes? What information is available on their site? What is your opinion of the site? Add your own concerns and insights to the list.

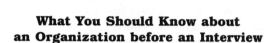

What You Should Know about
an Organization before an Interview

(Or, how do you know you would want to work there?)

1. Structure of organization (corporate, partnership, etc.)

2. Locations: main office, branches, overseas offices

3. Size of organization

4. Industry

5. Business

6. Product lines or services

7. How products or services are sold? E-commerce? Where sold (outlets/geographical)

8. Types of clients/customers; sales trends

9. Prices of products or services

10. Potential markets, products, services

11. History of organization: from inception to present

12. Ownership: public, private, or government

13. If public, growth, current price of stock, and where traded

14. Revenue and income history

15. Competitors

16. Management: who managers are and their backgrounds

17. Recent news stories about organization, industry, or management

18. Contacts in the industry or organization

19. Culture

20. Dress code/standards

21. Website

22. Public profile/reputation

After you have researched the basics, you should have insight into how the organization operates, who its competition is, how well it is doing, and how well it is thought of in the marketplace. Collectively, these diverse facts will help you to evaluate the organization's culture. Increasingly, in a job seeker's market (which existed for many in the late 1990s and continue to exist today), how and where you spend the greatest portion of your lifetime becomes a deciding factor in choosing an employer. Lifestyle and corporate culture are major factors in choosing the right employer (and for the organization hiring the right employee).

Getting Called Back

On round 2 of interviews, do the extra research. You and the organization are getting more serious.

❏ Find out about your interviewer; ask your networking resources or someone you know inside the organization; the first interviewer who recommended you may provide information about the next one such as how long he or she has been with the organization and current and prior assignments. You may look up the interviewer in *Who's Who*.

❏ Get inside the culture. Who are the main competitors? How are the products and services doing in the marketplace?

❏ Think of some original ways you might add value, based on your research.

❏ Would you buy/do you buy the company's products or services? Do you know someone who does?

Traditional and Online Research

To get to a win-win interview situation, you must determine your priorities, set your own timetable, and decide on your negotiating trade-offs. How can you do this without doing the requisite research into yourself and the job market? Where can you find the information that you need?

Start again with what you know. Do you know anyone who works or used to work at the organization? Or at a competing organization? In the same industry? This is the ideal time to do one-on-one research if you have a direct line to the organization. Contact the individual and be honest: *You want to apply for a job at XYZ, Inc.—can he or she help?* Be smart about whom you contact. A former employee who was downsized recently may not be the best person to set you up with the organization; likewise, someone who may not have your best interests at heart may do more harm than good.

Super Sources*

Americas Corporate Families
Directories in Print
Directory of Executive Recruiters
Encyclopedia of Associations
Marquis' Who's Who Series
Occupational Outlook Handbook
Standard & Poor's Directory of Corporations
Directors and Executives
U.S. Industrial Outlook

Publications
Crain's New York Business
The New York Times
Other major/local newspapers
Fast Company
Business 2.0
Industry Week
Business Week
Fortune
Inc.
Wired
Networking Magazine
Advertising Age
Forbes
Harvard Business Review
Information Week
Sloan Management Review
National Business Employment Weekly
The Wall Street Journal
Trade or industry journals
(See periodical Index for recent articles)

*many of these are available online.

Do you have a library card? If not, this may be the time to avail your-self of this free, local resource. There are many sources, both in print, on microfiche, or on tape, to assist you in your research. See the suggested "Super Sources" listing.

Electronic resources are a click away on the Internet. Constantly, or so it seems, new sites come up that offer many tools that a job seeker can use. Calendars, reminder services, free E-mail, and personalized news ser-vices are all available online. One of the newest (and most comprehensive) sites as of this writing is CEO Express (www.ceoexpress.com), a customiz-able business intelligence portal that includes links to major domestic and international newspapers, magazines, and industry resources as well as those links you wish to add personally. Free E-mail and connections to wireless devices as well as weather, travel, shopping, and an executive career center with links to job search sites, books, company and indus-try research, and even assistance when contemplating relocation are all available. Using one of these all-in-one, customizable sites as your home page will get you organized from the minute you log on. Another com-prehensive site is Wet Feet (wetfeet.com), which is specifically geared to job seekers. For interviewing help, visit the Job Interview Network (www.job-interview.net) where we are featured answering job interview questions.

What do Interviewers Look For?

Candidate is on time.

Candidate is neatly and appropriately dressed.

Candidate is prepared. He or she knows about us, about our industry and our product. Candidate knows what he or she has to offer us and backs up claims with examples.

Enthusiasm. Candidate appears friendly and interested in hearing more about the organization and the job.

Candidate is open and makes eye contact, is well spoken and confident.

Credibility. Interviewee is believable.

Candidate listens. He or she is able to understand our needs and goals.

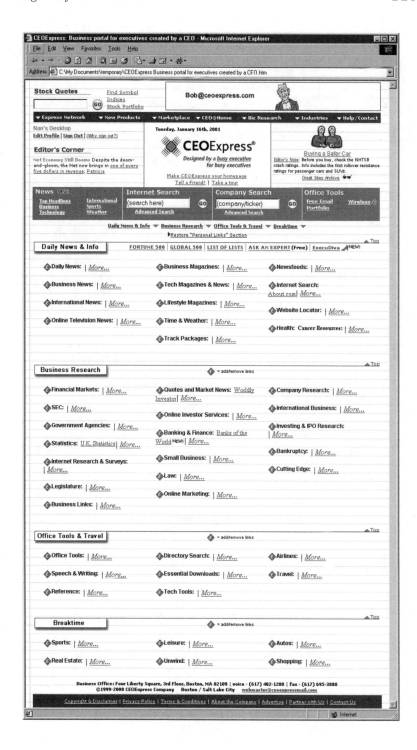

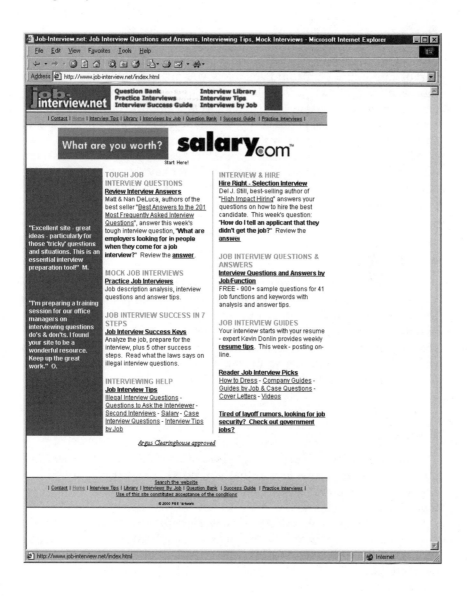

Focus

With your interview scheduled and your preparation done, the biggest part of your journey is behind you. Now you must maintain focus and enthusiasm for the interview itself. The evening or morning before the interview, review your notes and worksheets. Pack up your interview kit: recent résumés, notes, paper and pen, business cards, references list, and education and professional histories.

What areas of your work history or education do you feel the least confident about? Practice your responses and your key sales points. If you do not feel that you are a great candidate (if not the best candidate) for the position, how can you sell someone else on the idea?

Rehearse

If you have done the research, you now need to *rehearse*. Practice your responses to possible questions and have your agenda planned out. Ask a friend or family member to go over questions with you. **It is not enough to write down your answers!** You must get the sound and feel of them by speaking them out loud. You may hear mistakes or get suggestions from your audience. You do not want to memorize your answers—just be familiar with your probable responses.

Relax!

The purpose of the research is to give you ammunition for the interview; rehearsing should prove to you that you do know what you are talking about and that you are an excellent candidate. These factors should provide you with confidence.

But even the most seasoned interviewee or speaker can get stage fright or an anxiety attack before the event. You have been preparing, looking forward to doing well and "acing" the interview, do not undermine your own efforts!

Feeling stressed? Remind yourself:

You know the topic—yourself.

You are organized and prepared.

You are motivated. This is for you!

You have great material. You know your skills, you have examples to illustrate how you can do the job, and you have practiced.

Still shaky? Take a deep breath. Before you go into the building, take a walk to work off some (not all) of your excess energy. Find a quiet corner in the washroom to stretch or push against the wall to transfer your tension.

Practice, Practice, Practice

Whom are you meeting with? Do you know how to pronounce the organization's name and the name of the interviewer correctly? If you are uncertain, call the organization's main telephone number and inquire.

How will you get there? Unless you know the area very well, take a practice trip. Plan your route and allow for unforeseen delays.

What are you planning to wear? Choose your outfit in advance; check for needed cleaning, pressing, or repairs. Try the outfit sitting in different types of chairs; are you comfortable? If you scout out the organization physically ahead of time, see what the employees are wearing as they enter or exit the site. If informal dress code is apparent, dress slightly more formal.

Have a seat? Practice different seating arrangements—straight chair at a table, next to a desk, a comfy chair or two chairs next to each other. Where will you put your bag or purse? How will you take notes? Where can you put your folder? What should you do with your hands? Your feet?

Answers? Do you have them? Rehearse with a friend; practice giving short, concise responses. Tell stories to elaborate and add details. Time responses; none should be longer than 1 minute.

Questions? It is your turn to ask? Organize your questions by topics and make a written list. Practice asking questions and following up on the responses.

Pack up for the interview. Look like a pro. Use a folder or neat attaché case to bring extra copies of résumé, paper and pen, work samples, list of references, and details of work and education history (names, dates, addresses, and telephone numbers). Do not forget any articles you might need to freshen up if you are coming from work, another appointment, or a long commute.

Still nervous? Good. Adrenaline can carry you through! An aura of excitement and anticipation that does not incapacitate you will enhance that first impression. Dry off your hands and smile! Your nervousness is probably due to all you have invested in the process—the searching, writing the résumé, creating the marketing letter, the telephone calls, the research, and the rehearsing. What is the worst that will happen if you do not approach the interview with the utmost seriousness? Will you be hit with a laser and vanish from the face of the earth?

This is not a life-and-death situation; it is an interview, so lighten up. Enjoy it. Be passionate, eager, excited, and willing to invest in the process, but do not take it overly seriously. If this job does not come through, you will continue your job search and gain some perspective on the entire job search process. Care about the interview but do not care so much that you cannot enjoy it and do your best.

8

Back to Basics

Understanding the Interview Process

With the addition of E-mail, businesses receive hundreds of résumés weekly—some receive more than that daily—many of which are not even remotely related to the job openings available. Faxes and regular mail add piles more. Wading through those résumés, either by hand or using a database, to locate those few, select résumés that are probable candidates is a subjective process. When your résumé passes these hurdles, it makes the interview even more important. *Do not squander this opportunity,* whether you are unemployed or just comparison shopping. Treat every interview as an opportunity to present yourself in the best possible light and also to learn. To be a great interviewee you need the practice!

Dynamics of the interview

There are at least two definite agendas and possibly as many as four in the interview:

1. Your agenda
2. Interviewer's agenda
3. Hidden agenda—yours
4. Hidden agenda—the interviewer's

You may or may not have any insight into the interviewer's agenda. He or she may have a list of questions written down in advance, notes taken on your résumé, or certain details that are needed before the interview can really get under way. These items may be primary on the interviewer's agenda and must be satisfied before the interview can proceed to your agenda. These items are part of establishing rapport—being comfortable with each other and first allowing the interviewer to establish the pace and content of the interview.

In our other books we have said that interviewing is like dating, probably more like falling in love. It can be an intricate dance with signals sent back and forth. Part of your role is mirroring, or matching, the interviewer's pace, language, rhythm, and even body language.

You want the interview to progress to an easy give-and-take, business discussion format. Part of the burden of establishing this may fall on your shoulders. You have to be able to read the signals correctly. There is a level of reciprocity in an interview. The more the interviewer shares, the more you are expected to reveal. The more open you are, the more you may expect an equal level of candidness from the interviewer. If you respond candidly and the interviewer retreats to a more formal approach, you may then retreat also.

Like dating, if you get too friendly too soon, the other party may draw back. On the other hand, if you are approached in a friendly and interested manner and you do not reciprocate in kind, the interviewer may interpret your response to mean that you are not interested. It is extremely important to assess the situation correctly and respond in the appropriate manner. Your ability to do this in an interview is a key in-

What Do Interviewers Look For?

- ❏ Candidate is on time.
- ❏ Candidate is neatly and appropriately attired.
- ❏ Candidate is prepared. He or she knows about us, what industry and market we are in, and our products/services.
- ❏ Candidate knows what he or she has to offer us and backs up claims with examples.
- ❏ Candidate is enthusiastic. He or she appears friendly and interested in hearing more about the organization and the job.
- ❏ Candidate is open, makes eye contact; is well spoken and confident.
- ❏ Candidate is credible.
- ❏ Candidate listens. He or she is able to understand our needs and goals.

dicator of your interpersonal skills, something that an organization may consider essential to job performance. It is one thing to say, *"I am a people person"* and quite another to perform in an interview situation as a savvy, intuitive, and perceptive individual.

Your Agenda for the Interview

Regardless of the type of interview, what do you want the interviewer to learn from this interview? What are the points you plan to make? What do you want from this interview: a specific job, any job, a temporary job? What information do you need to know when the interview is over?

What about your hidden agendas? Do you need to prove that you can get the job offer, regardless of whether you are interested in the job or not? Are you trying to gather ammunition for a raise or transfer at your current job? Are you seeing if you are being paid the right amount now (and would you leave if offered more money)?

What Do They Need to Hear and Can You Say It?

After you have targeted an organization or a job opening, done your research, and determined that you wish to pursue this lead, you may be faced with alternatives not contemplated in an interview. The organization's culture, for example, may differ from that of its public persona. Not all the facets of an organization can be researched in advance, and surprises may be in store for you at the interview.

You need to have a clear sense of where you will draw the line in many areas of your job search. Which items are negotiable and which are not? When you can stretch the truth (*"Sure—I have used that computer program!"* meaning *"Well, I actually used it only once, and if need be I will certainly get proficient on it if I get this job."*) and when you can't (*"Certainly I am available for overtime"* while you are thinking (*"...well, Mondays I have my gym membership, Tuesday I usually pick up the kids at scouting, Wednesdays is . . ."*).

You need to have a clear sense of what you want and what you are willing to settle for. It is easy, in the heat of the moment, to agree to a work schedule that is less than ideal or to brag about accomplishments that are more than slightly exaggerated. Even worse than taking a job that is not what you want is having to go back and renege on your commitment and turn down the position. Know what you want and what you need before you walk into the interview; these parameters should be revisited regularly during your job search as the criteria may change with the introduction of reality. Additionally, as you visit different organizations, your preferences may change as well as your needs. Finances that were not an issue 2 months ago when you first became unemployed may now be more important. Before every interview, review your needs versus wants worksheet. Have your ideas changed? Are your goals still reasonable and realistic?

Interview Agenda
Take this with you on the interview.

Date of interview:

      How interview was obtained:

Organization:

Location:

Interviewer:

      Department/title:

Purpose of interview:

My agenda:

      Key points to make

1.

2.

3.

4.

      Key questions/issues to raise:

1.

2.

3.

4.

Recent magazine and newspaper articles cite another trend for job seekers. More and more candidates are being quoted as wanting jobs where "they can make a difference" and "where their contribution is valued." Employers that offer intrinsic values such as self-respect, job satisfaction, pride in the product or service, social rewards, ethics, and an opportunity to contribute are being actively sought. Do you work to live or live to work? Or, is it a combination? For some, employment provides the means to enjoy their personal life; for others, they seem to not have any personal life, so passionate are they about their careers.

Selling Yourself versus Selling (Yourself) Out

This is not meant to harken back to the idealism of the 1960s but rather the shooting-yourself-in-the-foot syndrome when words from your own mouth sell yourself out of the job. This can occur anywhere in an interview from the small-talk stage when you pass an innocuous comment about the performance record of the local sports team to the final goodbyes when you suddenly forget the name of the person you have been conversing with so intently for the past hour about your future. There are so many ways to make mistakes that other interviewees have surely made before you that there is no need for you to invent new ones. That is why a clear sense of purpose and preparation are keys to selling yourself into the job.

Disclosure versus Reciprocity and How Does the Truth Fit In

The military did not invent the "don't ask, don't tell" policy. It must have come out of the very first job interview! The interviewer knows that you are there to sell all your good points, to market yourself, and he or she expects a certain amount of hype. *"Leap tall or medium buildings in a single bound, did you say? Are you really faster than a locomotive ALL THE TIME?"* Even Superman would have his problems in a job interview.

You are selling your credibility. The interviewer needs to believe you. Legal issues revolving around job references leave many prior employers willing to just confirm dates of employment. You may be asked to bring in transcripts, salary statements, and names of current or past supervisors to corroborate your statements. If you are naturally humble in interviews, do not veer into self-deprecation; you could sell yourself out of the position. If you have any serious doubts, resolve them before the interview or *do not go*! If you do not think you are the person for the job, how can the interviewer think so? On the other hand, the hard sell, the "I can do anything" approach may appear unrealistic; the interviewer may not buy into it. Opt for a sensitive, open, and positive attitude and be honest in your answers. Be consistent and consider what your body language is saying: tightly crossed arms or legs, eye rolling, or filling in your answers with *"errr," "uhhh," and "like . . ."* can overshadow otherwise great answers. So can using words three sizes too large; if they are not part of your normal vocabulary or if you are unsure of the meaning, do not take them to the interview!

You control disclosure. You have structured a résumé geared to present you in the best light. You have highlighted your key selling points in your marketing letter. In an interview, you need not offer information that is not included in your résumé unless it will support your candidacy. One example is your annual vacation. Here it is early March, and you are interviewing for a position with a mid-April starting date. Every year you have taken a 3-week vacation in August with your family and coordinated the dates with your daughter's need to be driven to college. You have to book your condo six months in advance, which you have already done. Do you mention this in regard to discussions about when you are available to start work? No. This is a subject that can be discussed later, when there is a firm job offer and when salary and other benefits are negotiated. Yet job applicants suffer pangs of worry and concern that they are being dishonest in these early interviews.

Establish reciprocity. There should be a rhythm, a give-and-take attitude in the interview. Common ground is established early during the small talk or warm-up segment. Then topics change, and more information is shared. As you reveal more of yourself during the interview, there is an expectation on your part that your candidness will be rewarded with similar forthrightness on the part of the interviewer. Since you are both in a selling situation, you both should be interested in showing your "product" in the best light and highlighting all the most attractive features.

Profile of an Interview

You are prepared. You have revisited the organization's Website and reviewed your notes. You have rehearsed the tough questions; you have looked over the copies of the résumé and marketing letter you sent. If

Interviewing Basics

❏ **Schedule interviews intelligently.** Try not to be the first person inter-viewed. Avoid Monday mornings, Friday afternoons, or late in the day.

❏ **Dress as if you work there already.** A well-groomed and organized candidate makes a great first impression.

❏ **Have fresh copies of your résumé** (the one that you submitted to the organization) available. Reread it beforehand.

❏ **Bring your Education and Work History** worksheets in case you need details to complete an application. Have your Social Security Card and identification (driver's license, passport) with you.

❏ **Have names and addresses for references** with you, if needed. Arrive on time which means 15 minutes before the appointment.

❏ **Be nice.** A positive, cheerful attitude is contagious.

❏ **Show sincere interest** by a firm handshake and smile.

❏ **Be calm and clear-spoken.** Be "up" for the interview; use adrenaline to work for you.

❏ **You have always worked with and for winners.** Do not make negative comments about former or current employers.

❏ **Listen.** Use the pauses and silences. Think before you speak. Take notes (but ask permission first).

❏ **Use the interviewer's name** during the interview.

❏ **Believe you are the best candidate.** Sell your best points.

❏ **Ask questions.** Get the information you need to make the decision. Do you want to work there? Do you want this job?

❏ **Understand the hiring procedure.** What is the next step? When will a decision be made?

❏ **Ask for the job.** If you want it, let the interviewer know. Don't make him or her guess or assume that you are interested. Close with strong reasons why you are the solution to the problems.

❏ **Follow up—always.** Send a thank-you note immediately.

❏ **Debrief yourself.** Outline the interview for yourself. What parts went well? Where did you feel you could have done better? How was the in-terviewer? What did you think of the organization? Is there anything else to do?

❏ **Assess your chances.** Do you think you will get an offer? Why or why not?

there was an ad, you have reviewed it. You have done the research, you are dressed appropriately, and your qualifications are impeccable. You are not only on time, you are 15 minutes early to allow yourself time to freshen up. Looking at maps and schedules (whether online or in the traditional manner) you know your travel route and approximate time of arrival. Because you planned your route in advance, you were able to find the office easily. You are bringing several fresh copies of your résumé as well as several recent writing or work samples, and you have reviewed them one last time to check for any inconsistencies or errors. You have a small pad of paper and a pen to write with (leave the promotionally inscribed pens home; use a ballpoint, rollerball or fountain pen).

As you approach the building, you notice what the neighborhood is like. As you enter the offices, you take mental note of the surroundings and any employees whom you see. What are the furnishings like? What are the vibes that you pick up: is this an organization you could imagine being part of? Take mental note of any amenities that are of particular interest (parking facilities, for example).

Be nice to everyone you meet. Listen for the name of the person with whom you will be meeting if you did not know in advance. Ask for the spelling of the name if you are not certain of the pronunciation. When you are introduced to your interviewer, rise (if you are seated) and shake hands firmly (unless this is not your custom) and use the interviewer's name. "I am so pleased to meet you, Mr./Mrs./Ms. _____." Before the end of the meeting ask for his or her business card if one is not offered, when convenient; if you have one, offer yours in exchange.

Where are you being interviewed? In a conference room, a cubicle, or the interviewer's office? Take mental notes about surroundings; this can indicate importance paid to the human elements in an organization. What is the privacy factor? Has the door been closed to reduce interruptions? There is a funny scene in the film *The Big Picture* where Kevin Bacon comes to sell his directing talents to the hot-shot producer, J. T. Walsh. J. T. tells his secretary to, *"Hold all calls—this is a very important meeting."* He then proceeds to jump up and answer the telephone at any opportunity as well as cut the meeting short for another meeting he has scheduled. This happens despite assuring Kevin that *"my time is yours."* His words were geared to making Kevin feel important, but his actions did not.

There will be a certain amount of polite small talk—the weather, your ability to find the office easily. Stay away from any possible controversial topics, including political events or the performance of last night's local sports team. You can never be certain on what side of an issue an interviewer stands and whether it makes any difference to your candidacy.

First Impressions

Too often the first impression is not deemed important enough to prepare for, but these crucial first minutes are when the interviewee makes the often unalterable first impression! This is also the time to build rapport with the interviewer, to establish credibility, and to find a common ground.

This is another two-way evaluation. You may be so concerned in the first few minutes with the effect that you are having on the interviewer, you may not allow the interviewer's impression to register with you. What is noticed by most interviewers in the first 7 seconds?

❑ *Energy level:* Are you giving off an air of excitement or one of uncertainty and trepidation? Do you look and act like you are happy and excited to be there?

❑ *Appropriateness:* Are your dress and demeanor in sync with the organization? Do you look like you could be working there already?

❑ *Consistency:* No surprises. You look and sound like your résumé and cover letter. Do you match the claims in your marketing package, such as high energy, proactive, hands-on, and great people skills?

❑ *Confidence:* Do you project self-assurance, professionalism, and a sense of the role?

The Questions

We said in *201 Answers* that there are only four categories of questions in any interview:

1. *"Oh, I am so glad you asked"* (this is what I really want you to know).

2. *"Uh-oh. You do not want to go there"* (illegal questions).

3. *"Ouch! I was really hoping you would not ask about that!"* (all those sensitive, uncomfortable areas).

4. *"Oh my! I never thought of that"* (questions you never anticipated).

The only way to prepare for any of these questions is to *practice.* Consider all the possible questions that you could be asked and have cogent responses for them. It is not enough to read these questions and answers (even the ones in our books). It is not enough to write out your answers in advance (which is a good idea). This is a spoken exercise—practice saying your answers out loud. Ask a friend or relative to do a Q & A session with you; ask for their feedback. You want to sound comfortable with your answers—not rehearsed. You want to have information (dates, places, work assignments) well in mind. You want to be able to concentrate on those questions that require you to think carefully about your answers.

The Closing

What are some of the telltale signs that the interviewer considers the interview over, short of escorting you bodily to the door?

❏ *Body language:* The interviewer looks at his or her watch, stands up, or sits up straight. Walking and opening the door is another obvious sign.

❏ *Questions: "Is there anything else you wish to discuss?" "Do you have any further questions?"*

Keeping the Interview on the Right Track

❏ Be helpful with your responses but do not inject any negative comments about yourself or others.

❏ Do not be afraid to say those three little words, "*I don't know*" or "*Nothing comes to mind at the moment*"; follow up (if you can) with ". . . *but I can find out.*"

❏ Think of headlines when you tell your (short) stories. Get their attention with the results ("*I cut overhead 12 percent*"). Follow with why this was important ("*There were enormous expenses with starting a new product line*") and then finish with the cliffhanger: how you accomplished this feat!

❏ Don't stay in the dark. If you do not understand the question, ask. "*If I understand you correctly, you want to know what I would do if . . . ?*" or "*I am not certain I understand the question completely. Could you rephrase it?*"

❏ Take your measure as you go—ask for some feedback, "*Am I providing enough information?*" or, "*Am I giving you the information you need?*"

❏ Need to make a point but were not asked? Do not be afraid to insert it yourself into the conversation. "*When I was reading about your organization, I remembered a time when . . . .*"

Thank the interviewer by name for his or her time and information. Unless stated previously, find out what the next step will be. Should you call back? When will a decision be made? Is there anything else that is needed to be done?

Last-Minute Warnings

- ❑ **Don't smoke, chew gum, or drink** during the interview, even if you are invited to. You do not need another thing to worry about (spills, ashes, alcohol).
- ❑ **Don't bring friends or relatives.** If they come along, meet them afterward in the coffee shop.
- ❑ **Don't admit to flaws.** We all know we all have them, but this is supposed to be your sales call. Stress the positives.
- ❑ **Don't whine.** Bringing up problems in old jobs, your personal life, or with the job search brings too much negativity into the interview.
- ❑ **Don't say how much you need this job.** It is immaterial to the selection process, and the interviewer really does not want to get into issues of your mortgage, divorce settlement, or college tuition payments.
- ❑ **Don't drop names.** If you have been referred, the interviewer should know this from your cover letter or prior conversations; there is no need to sprinkle names into the conversation. You can reek of elitism or annoy the interviewer (you just mentioned a foe).
- ❑ **Don't look at your watch.** Unless asked to extend your visit, your time is the interviewer's because this meeting is that important to you.
- ❑ **Don't be a one-man (or woman) band.** Add some "we's" into your stories—teamwork is highly valued.
- ❑ **Don't forget to be yourself and enjoy** meeting this person and hearing about the organization and job.
- ❑ **Don't forget to ask for the job and thank the interviewer for the time.**
- ❑ **Don't forget to ask what the next step(s) will be.**

If you are really interested in this position, say so. Many an interviewer is left wondering whether he or she has made a positive impression on the candidate and whether the candidate would accept if the job were offered. Do not leave ambiguity in your wake. *"Based on everything we have discussed this morning, Ms. Durkin, I am more interested in ABC, Inc., now than I was when I arrived. I feel that my experience in ___ makes me a very strong candidate. I look forward to speaking with you in the next week/few days/____."*

Questions

8.1 Everybody has pet peeves. What are yours?

This is a variation of the "What are your weaknesses or dislikes" questions. Treat it as such. Remember, you are not answering a psychologist or a Franz Kafka disciple performing research. Think of something that has positive overtones, such as *"I really dislike seeing any employee give less than 100 percent."* Or, *"I really dislike seeing office supplies being wasted."* Another is, *"Needless expenses."* You get the idea.

8.2 Give me an example of a time you had a conflict with the customer.

The customer was annoyed that her sight line from the seat provided for a performance was obstructed by unruly fans. I wasn't sure she was telling the truth or just hoping for some free tickets. Even though I suspected, I wasn't sure, so I offered her two free seats the next time we were in town.

8.3 Give me an example of a time you had an idea for an improvement.

The company was wasting money going outside for reception coverage. The only advantage was that this provided a ready pool of backups. As a cost-effective alternative, I suggested that our department would take responsibility for reception coverage. I would get one additional staff member but would also provide backup. I made this suggestion only after I made the suggestion to the members of my staff to see how they felt about the idea. They bought into it even though it meant more work for them. I then went to senior management and got their approval. Since we made the switch, the last two receptionists (both college graduates) stayed within the organization and started up career ladders.

8.4   *What was your greatest accomplishment while in your current (or earlier) job?*

The seamless move of the sales office from one location to the other—3 percent under budget and on time.

The systematic, 5 percent reduction in staff in a respectful, cost-effective manner—and with no lawsuits.

The negotiation of a new insurance contract with better coverage at the same cost.

9
Interview Problems

Even if you are prepared and ideal for the job, the interview may not go as you would hope. An interview is a conversation with a purpose—the purpose ostensibly being to hire you! However, that may not always be the case. You have your agenda: the points you wish to make in the interview, the questions you need answered, and the job offer you want to get. What is the interviewer's agenda? What is the purpose of this interview from his or her point of view?

How the Employer/
Interviewer Sees You
and Why

Most likely, the interviewer really wants to hire you. It would make his or her life much easier to fill the vacancy quickly and inexpensively with the right hire. The interviewer would like to include you even while asking you questions to see if you should be excluded.

If you are being interviewed in a personnel or human resources department, the chances are that there will be a list of requirements that will have to be satisfied before you can proceed in the interviewing process. Job experience, education, and skill set will be looked at closely. The interviewer may or may not have an understanding or working knowledge of the job opening. He or she may or may not have a complete or up-to-date job description. There may or may not even be a 'real' job opening! Not a real job opening? Then why are you there? The organization may have identified another candidate and is just confirming its choice.

If you are being interviewed by a line manager or department head, someone actively involved in the day-to-day operations of the department where you would be working, that individual is more likely to look into your potential. He or she will be more open to seeing the possibilities of someone who may not fit every requirement on paper. Since she or he would be someone whom you would work with, personalities and chemistry count for more (although an interviewer in HR might inexplicably like or dislike you.)

Then there is the total *subjectivity* of the process. You have no idea of the candidates who have preceded you or who will follow. You cannot know the internal politics of the hiring process, the miserable commute to work the interviewer had this morning, or the fact that this is his or her last week at work and is leaving for another job! There are controllable factors—your résumé, your presentation, your credentials, and your responses—but there are many more uncontrollable factors present in the interview. When there are problems during an interview, they may have nothing to do with you. Accept this fact and your anxiety level will fall.

Legal Issues

You may be unsure about the legality of questions raised in an interview or sensitive to questions that appear intrusive. Employers are prohibited under Title VII of the Civil Rights Act of 1964 from discrimination in employment (including hiring and firing) based on race, creed, color, national origin, and sex. Some states have expanded this to include sexual orientation and marital status.

The organization can ask about certain issues, such as whether you have ever been convicted of a crime (you may be asked to provide details); whether you have permission to work in this country; what you were doing during periods of unemployment of 3 months or more (they may ask for someone to verify your whereabouts). The organization may also ask if you ever were given a garnishment; if there are reasons you can't work Saturdays or Sundays (this should be asked only if the job requires you to work weekends). It is also legal to ask you to provide a copy of your pay statement from your past employer or a copy of last year's tax return (commonly asked of salespeople). The organization may also ask you for a home address and telephone number (it may legally refuse to accept only a post office box number address). It is also legal to subject you to a drug test, if one is given to all applicants. If you do not like an employer who is making what you feel are intrusions into your private life, then you should question whether you want to establish a relationship with this organization.

Classic Problems that Can Affect Anyone

Even though you have done everything possible to prepare for this interview, problems may still arise. If you truly have done your homework and are prepared, you can make the best of a seemingly poor situation. Although the subject is covered in detail in our previous book, every candidate should be aware of illegal questions. These may be areas that concern you. Know that they may not be asked. But if they are asked, you may choose to answer if you think it will help your candidacy. You may also offer the information freely if you are not asked.

Following are some of the situations a candidate could face in an interview, from the sublime to the ridiculous.

Illegal Interview Topics

Any questions regarding:

       Race

       Color

       Religion

       National origin

       Sex (including pregnancy)

       Age (40 years or older)

These are all prohibited by federal law.

Also protected under other legislation:

       Disability

       Vietnam era veterans

       Disabled veterans

       Arrest records

       Garnishments

       Bankruptcy

Additionally, some states prohibit questions regarding marital status and/or sexual orientation.

Situation: The interviewer is obviously unprepared for this interview and has no idea who you are or why you are there.

Did you call to confirm this interview within the past 24 hours? If you are certain you are where you are supposed to be, help the interviewer out. Do not make the interviewer feel insecure by making a point of his or her lack of preparation. Remind the interviewer of who you are, what job you are interviewing for, and how you came to be referred to the organization. Offer a fresh copy of your résumé.

Thank you for seeing me about the _____ (position) in your _____ department. Ms. _____ (recruiter) said she had spoken to you last week and forwarded my résumé to your department. Here is a fresh copy if you would like to see it. And I have attached some additional information about projects I have currently worked on. Is this still a good time to meet?

Situation: The interviewer is all talk, talk, and talk! You can hardly get a word in about your candidacy. It is more of a lecture than an interview.

Pick a point where you can logically turn the subject to something you need to know.

You certainly have given me a lot of information about ABC Company. You must have been here for a while. Does the company have a lot of turnover?

Feed off the interviewer's comments to make a point about your background.

Now that you mentioned it, I was really interested in _____ because at my previous employer, I was involved in _____. What is the size of the current department?

If everything you try fails, hope that your being a good listener will get you passed to the next level of interviews.

Situation: The interview hardly gets under way, and it is one interruption after another. The telephone rings, there are knocks on the door, and the fax machine is rattling away.

I see that you are very busy today. Is there a more convenient time you would like to continue this interview?

If this afternoon is no longer convenient, I certainly would be willing to reschedule.

This attitude gives the interviewer a slight nudge (if he or she has any perception) that you are willing to continue the interview but that it is hard to do so with all the interruptions.

Interruptions can work to your advantage providing they are not so numerous as to prohibit any conversation. First of all, the interviewer may feel guilty about all these interruptions and thus may feel more kindly to your candidacy. Second, after each interruption you have the ability to take control of the interview: *"As I was about to say in response to your question . . ." "I was just going to comment on a situation that happened recently that may interest you . . . ."* Furthermore, eavesdropping is hard to avoid when you are sitting right there, and you may pick up on some details that could give you insight into the organization. However, do not get so interested in the interruption that you lose your train of thought!

Situation: You arrived on time for your interview and are kept waiting for over 30 minutes.

How long is long enough to wait? If you are being told that the interviewer is aware that you are waiting and is being held up by another meeting or an event out of his or her control, you could decide to wait further or reschedule. A 15–20 minute delay certainly can happen; waiting for over 30 minutes seems excessive unless the circumstances are unusual or extraordinary. If there is no word and you have no idea whether the interviewer knows you are waiting (he or she is not in the office, and no one seems to know where he or she is), waiting for 15 minutes and then leaving word that you are willing to reschedule is a reasonable tactic.

> *It looks like Ms. C is caught up in a meeting. I do not want to rush through the interview; please let her know I appreciate her situation, and I will call later to reschedule.*
>
> *I was looking forward to meeting with Mr. D at 3 P.M. but, since it is growing so late and I have other appointments, please advise him that I cannot wait any longer. Can I reschedule another meeting time through you?*
>
> *I was hoping to meet with Mrs. D for our 4:40 interview, but she seems to be detained somewhere. Can I leave a message with you for her to contact me to arrange another time to meet? Due to other arrangements, I cannot wait any longer.*

Situation: You accepted a job with another organization and now have a better offer.

There are two thoughts on this.

1. How good is your word? If you have carefully considered the first offer before accepting it, are you going to be happy with yourself if you follow the dollar?

2. Offers extended by employers can be rescinded—don't you have the same right? The price would be that you would not be able (easily) to go back down that road again with the first employer.

Situation: You are 8 months pregnant and definitely look it. What should you say in the interview?

Legally, interviewers cannot ask about your pregnancy but you know it is on their mind. Bring it up yourself!

> *Since you cannot help but notice that I am very pregnant, I want to assure you that I take my career very seriously and have made child-care plans in advance, as I did with my other children. Other than a short hospital stay, I will not miss any assignments and can fully commit to this position. If my former employer had not moved out of state, I would have continued my employment there.*

What if you are only 2 months pregnant and do not show at all? That is a personal situation; questions about your marital and parental status are illegal. Six or seven months down the road you will have passed any trial period and can make the appropriate arrangements with your employer. If you are feeling guilty about not saying anything, just ask yourself *"Would a man about to become a father warn his soon-to-be employer that he would be asking for parental leave in 6 months?"*

Situation: It's only 5 minutes into the conversation, and you are getting very bad feelings about this interview. The interviewer is definitely not interested in you or your candidacy; it feels as if you are actually resented or disliked, and you have no idea why.

The interviewer can just be having a bad day and the problem has nothing to do with you. You may look like someone he or she knew and disliked immensely. The interviewer just left a meeting where he or she was chewed out and is feeling very edgy and vulnerable. You attended University X, the archrival of his or her alma mater, University Y. He or she could have literally gotten up on the wrong side of the bed and is hungry, irritable, and lacking the grace to not bring these feelings into the interview. It may just be an outward sign of withdrawal in one more attempt to quit smoking.

Follow the interviewer's lead and let him or her establish the tone and pace of the interview. Perhaps working through his or her agenda will help establish rapport. Keep the startled-deer look out of your eyes and the frozen smile off your lips; maintain a calm, pleasant demeanor in the hope that the situation will reveal itself or at least not worsen. By offering your best, you are doing the best you can with what may be an unfixable situation.

Situation: The interviewer tells you, "The job is all but filled. I am seeing you because it was too late to cancel the interview with you."

Keep your name in the running by still selling yourself; you never know if the other candidate will accept the position or if another one will open up that would suit you even better.

> *I am pleased to hear that your search is coming to an end, but I hope the door is not completely closed. I feel that my _____ (key selling points) uniquely qualify me for the position of _____.*

Situation: The interviewer acts extremely nervous and inexperienced, does not make eye contact, and fidgets constantly with papers on the desk.

Part of your role as interviewee is to help the interviewer learn why you are the best candidate for the position. Some interviewers may need more help than others, and you may have a greater responsibility in establishing rapport. Think about how nervous you were. Here is someone terrified of you! Put all those "people" skills you mentioned on your résumé into action! Point the interviewer in the right direction—the job you want!

> *I am very glad to be able to meet with you today Mr. _____. Here is a recent copy of my résumé. As you can see by the points I outlined in my summary, I have the experience as well as the technical skills to move into the position of _____.*

You might try drawing the interviewer out a bit further into the conversation.

> *There has been a lot happening in the ____ industry lately. Have you been with ABC Company long?*
>
> *I have spent ___ years in _____(profession); have you always been in the personnel/human resources/department ____?*

Ask a general question about the organization.

Has ABC Company always been located here in _____?

If these gambits do not warm up or relax the interviewer, just press on and make as many key selling points as you can.

Situation: Despite all your planning, there was a four-alarm fire near your house which blocked your car; consequently you arrived 15 minutes late for your interview.

You are not the first one to be caught up in a situation you cannot control despite your best intentions. Make a short explanation and offer to reschedule.

You might see my neighborhood on the 11 o'clock news because of the fire emergency. This is why I was unavoidably detained, and I apologize. If you would like to meet at another time, I would certainly be happy to reschedule and promise to keep my windows open listening for sirens the next time!

Situation: While you are riding up in the elevator to your interview, a deli delivery person spilled coffee on you and there is nothing you can do about it.

Make light of the situation. Acknowledge what happened briefly and then move on to the interview, showing grace under pressure.

Pleased to meet you. I had no idea elevators attacked applicants! If you promise not to notice the coffee stains I received on the way up courtesy of a hurried delivery person, I will promise to forget about them myself. I will pretend that I am as fresh as I was when I left my home for this interview.

Situation: You felt confident and relaxed until you met your interviewer. Suddenly, your voice is shaky, and you have gotten a bad case of nerves. You know the interviewer notices your nervousness by your sweaty handshake.

Gather your wits and make a fresh start. Take a silent, deep, calming breath and remind yourself of all the positive elements in your candidacy. Then move on to the interview.

It is a pleasure to meet with you. I have been thinking about this interview for so long that I really should not be this nervous at all but a little adrenaline is good. In fact, this morning I was reading about ____ (name something related to industry, organization) which made me even more interested in the possibility of working for XYZ Company."

Situation: You survived the interview, but just barely; you feel
you made a poor impression and that the interviewer was totally
lacking in interviewing skills. You still want the job despite this
person's performance.

Remember David Letterman's mother's performance during the
Olympics, especially when she interviewed Hillary Clinton? She was so
nervous that she was doing a terrible interview but Hillary—love her or
hate her—was the most gracious interviewee and in the process made
David's mother look better while she showed what a classy person she
was as well. The result was a win-win for all concerned. The point is to
not give up while the interview is still going on—even as it is winding
down. There are stories we all hear about someone going out the door
with a terrible interview finally over and a casual comment grabs the
interviewer's ear. The situation is salvaged right on the brink. This does
not happen that often.

If the interview ends and there is no redemptive opportunity, still do
not give up. Don't bet the ranch on a positive outcome but continue to be
courteous and act professionally—long after the interview is over and
with whomever you come into contact. Send that thank-you note and
make comments bringing out points that you felt you were never able to
emphasize (or discuss at all). Maybe the interviewer has stronger written
communication skills and will relate better to something in writing.

Stress: When and Why Do You Feel It for a Job Interview?

Reticence in meeting new people, becoming involved in unknown situations, and having to present your qualifications for inspection can trigger
a bout of shyness in many job candidates. How does this shyness mani-
fest itself? Sweaty palms, mumbling voice, a tremble in the handshake, or
averted glances can all but undo an otherwise qualified candidate in an
interview.

If you are just a natural worrier, cut down your stress level by being
thoroughly prepared. Do not skimp on going over your prior jobs, skills,
and experience. For example, if you have been doing temp work for a
while, mentally review every assignment and list the organization,
whom you reported to, and what the job entailed; associate the skills
you used on these jobs with the skills you will need for the job you are
seeking.

Temp Worksheet

List your assignments, most recent first, with the details of each. Note responsibilities and experience; if there was a significant accomplishment or new skill learned, note this in the Comments section.

Assignment at_____ Dates: _____

Contact/supervisor: _____ Phone: _____

Job/responsibilities: _____

Comments: _____

* * * * * *

Assignment at_____ Dates: _____

Contact/supervisor: _____ Phone: _____

Job/responsibilities: _____

Comments: _____

* * * * * *

Assignment at_____ Dates: _____

Contact/supervisor: _____ Phone: _____

Job/responsibilities: _____

Comments: _____

* * * * * *

Assignment at_____ Dates: _____

Contact/supervisor: _____ Phone: _____

Job/responsibilities: _____

Comments: _____

* * * * * *

Assignment at_____ Dates: _____

Contact/supervisor: _____ Phone: _____

Job/responsibilities: _____

Comments: _____

* * * * * *

Handling Stress

What causes you the most concern? Do you feel that you will stumble and trip as you are introduced? Burp instead of giving a succinct answer? Or is your greatest fear "clamming up" and being ramrod-straight and unresponsive?

Take a cue from performers and visualize yourself being successful in the interview. Paint a mental picture of yourself calm, confident, and with all your wits about you as you are interviewed. Remember all the time you spent doing research and rehearsing. Call to mind your achievements and prior successes.

If stress is your continual companion in your interviews, try getting more exercise—particularly on the day before your interview. This will help to tire you out and enable you to get a good night's sleep. Do a light workout—a brisk walk perhaps—the morning of the interview, and you will feel physically great. You are a great candidate for this position—you just need to let the interviewer know it!

Unique Problems

Beyond those situations that can happen to us all, there are circumstances that are unique to many candidates—and some may fall into more than one category. These circumstances are revealed in their professional or educational histories.

❑ Changing from temp work to full-time or part-time work or vice versa

❑ Foreign-educated

❑ Fired or terminated after probation period

❑ Prison or felony record

❑ Ran your own business; bankruptcy

❑ Serial absences due to work-related illness

❑ Filed harassment claim(s) (or other legal issues pending) against former employer

❑ Special working arrangement needed (hours or days)

❑ Foreign worker or returning expatriate

Keep in mind that you are not the first (or the last) to be in this situation; interviewers have heard it all before and worse. The only element that you can control is how you deal with it. Make it a big problem, and this is how it will be perceived. Remember that you have the right to control disclosure. (Remember all those threats in school about what is in your permanent record?)

Stress the positives. Acknowledge the problem if it comes up and establish your past successes as well as your plans for future achievements. See the answers to the questions for examples.

Questions

Temporary Assignments

9.1 Why did you work as a temp for 4 years? Why did you start temping?

I was hoping to make a career as a theatre/film/TV artist, so I started temping to keep a flexible schedule and have a steady income at the same time. This temporary situation lasted more than 4 years, but now I realize that I am not going to become a star so I am concentrating my attention on my business career instead.

My children were young so I only worked mornings while they were in school. Now that they are older, I can commit to full-time employment.

9.2 Why do you want to now work for a company as a regular employee?

I realize there are real advantages to being an employee with benefits and a relationship with a company instead of being a "hired hand."

9.3 Why are you leaving regular employment for temping?

I really want to give the artistic part of me some attention, and I see temping as a more flexible arrangement that will allow me to make and keep commitments (such as casting calls) as they come up without compromising my status (and security) as a temporary employee.

9.4 What kinds of assignments did you have as a temp that relate to the work here at our organization?

Most recently, my assignment for the past 7 weeks has been to input data into a database for a new furniture sales Website. I used ____ software, which I had not used before, but it was similar to ____, which I have used. Before that, I was involved in analyzing and creating charts for a marketing company. Since this job opening involves both analysis and data input, I feel that I do have the experience required.

9.5 *What kinds of temporary or freelance assignments do you want?*

This is another version of, "Why do you want to work here?" and "What can you do for us?" Give your responses accompanied by reasons why you are qualified.

I had done a lot of telephone fund-raising for my children's school and really enjoyed the experience. And I was great at getting donations. Telemarketing would have the flexibility that I am looking for, and I feel that I would be doing something that I both enjoy and seem to be good at.

9.6 *Where have you worked lately? Why didn't one of these companies offer you a job? Why didn't you try for a job at one of them?*

Actually, I have contacted my last two supervisors about positions, but both organizations are outsourcing many activities and are continuing to rely on temps to fill in. They did say they would contact me if the situation changes, but, in the meantime, they would be pleased to recommend me.

Foreign-Educated

9.7 *I see you went to school overseas; why did you not attend school in the United States?*

In my senior year of high school I was accepted at several universities in the United States, but _____ University in Milan offered me a generous scholarship as well as the opportunity to use the Italian I had acquired in my classes. I felt this was a tremendous opportunity to study art while being able to see the originals.

My parents were in the military stationed in Germany; it was a logical choice for me.

9.8 *How do _____ schools compare with those in the United States? What school in the United States do you feel is comparable?*

You want to point out that you made a wise decision in your choice of schooling without appearing arrogant or elitist in your thinking.

Since I had wanted to study _____, any school that had an international faculty and student body would have been a possibility. As it was, the University of _____ had a comprehensive curriculum and many of the students in attendance were also Americans. Not only did I get a great education, I now know people in my field of study all over the world. The larger universities in major cities that attract foreign students, such as _____ (names of schools) would also have been great choices but the opportunity to study in _____ was too great to pass up.

9.9 Do you feel that you got a good education there?

It was a more evenly paced, less competitive atmosphere and there seemed to be an honest love of learning that permeated the faculty. Not only did I gain knowledge in the field of _____, I was able to interact and be effective with students and faculty from different cultures and points of view. That part of my education is invaluable to me.

9.10 How does a diploma/certificate from _____ compare to one from a U.S. school?

Based on the courses taken and grading system, my diploma/certificate is equal to a _____ degree in _____ as issued by an American school. In fact, should I choose to attend graduate school, virtually all of my credits would be recognized by most major U.S. universities.

Fired or Terminated

Important advice: Before any discussion of reasons why you left a former employer, find out the official version of your leaving. What will the company say, if contacted? Since most employers only confirm dates of employment, specifics of your performance and termination are usually not discussed. However—and this is a big however—there are informal discussions among peers, and you may not know what is common knowledge. Chances are, the higher up you were in the organization, the more notice was taken of your departure. Gossip and a small-town atmosphere can permeate many industries, and the details surrounding your leaving may have been passed around, whether they are correct or not. If this is a concern, get the lowdown from friends and peers before you commit yourself to a story that can be easily contradicted. The best tack to take is the truth—or a version of it from your point of view.

Whether you have been justly or unjustly terminated (or fired or let go or downsized or canned—whatever the euphemism) leave all your hurt feelings, anger, and recriminations outside the interview! Even though it may be difficult, put forward the thought that you were always associated with winners.

9.11 Were you ever fired or terminated?

There it is—asked right up front. You can use several euphemisms such as, *"I was downsized,"* or *"I was let go."* Do not get into the blame game. Unless you or your manager made the front pages, the less said about details, the better off you will be. However, you can admit that politics played a role.

> *My manager hired his new son-in-law to replace me.*
> *The president's daughter was placed in charge of the unit instead of me.*

You cannot be faulted for another's capricious management decision. Just do not elaborate on how much of a boob the relative was or how you heard that the department is headed downhill since you left.

9.12 What was your greatest mistake?

If you were fired for cause and this is the official story, look on the bright side: you have your answer. Briefly state what the mistake was and how you resolved the issue. Explain the lesson you learned and how it has made you better for it. Then move on to a positive point.

> *The importance of operating manuals was never impressed on me. After this unfortunate incident, I have become religious about reading any manuals issued and keeping them up to date.*
> *Although I apologized to the customer for losing her order, company policy dictated that I be released from service. This job search has reinforced my dedication to following through on all telephone calls and directions.*

9.13 Why did you leave after only 3 months (or a comparable short period of time)?

Well, why did you? What is closest to the truth? If you stay within the truth, you will not be nervous or contradict yourself in the interview; if you are called back for a follow-up interview, you will not forget what your answer was if you adhere to the truth.

> *The job did not turn out to be as it was described to me.*
> *The organization changed its focus (or goals).*
> *Despite the information exchanged in the interview, the organization could not effectively use my skills and talents.*
> *There really was not enough work for me to do; too much down time.*
> *There was a change in management and the new group wanted to bring in its own staff.*

The area was scheduled for a downsizing (or reorganization) and since I was the most recent hire, I planned accordingly.

It just did not work out.

All these will probably prompt a follow-up question. Do not fabricate. Most interviewers have heard these stories before and really are not interested in all the gory details. (Note that a job of several months' duration need not be included on your résumé, but it may have to be included on an application form in order to account for all your time.)

Circumstances also come into play . . . . Did you leave your other job to take this four month job? Or did you 'try' it while already unemployed . . . hoping for the best? If you were recruited to change jobs, there is a lot of room for exaggeration in a sales pitch, and many employees have been misled.

When I was recruited for this position it was with the understanding that I would not be required to travel. This turned out to not be the case. As soon as they were able to replace me I left; there was no other comparable job in the organization to move into.

If you have held other jobs for substantial periods and you took the other job in good faith, stress your past performance. You are not a capricious person—you have lived up to your commitments in the past. You have skills to offer and want to put them to good use.

9.14 Why did you leave your last job without a new job to move into?

Unless one of the above reasons fits your circumstances, you must look further for your truth.

I thought I had another job lined up; there was a job offer that I had accepted. I had given the company 3 weeks' notice and took a week's vacation. Two days before I was to report to work, I was notified that the organization had chosen not to expand its product line, and my presence was not needed.

The company had grown stale and there really was nothing further for me to do. Leaving was a serious decision, and looking for a new job is extremely important—something that I felt deserved my full attention. It did not seem fair to my other employer to take long lunches or keep coming in late because of my job search.

Management recently chose an operating style that did not suit me. Since I knew major changes were coming, I felt it was wiser to make the change myself.

These responses can open the door to follow-up questions; be prepared to look for the other shoe falling! A great follow-up question to the above reason would be, "What style of management do you prefer to work with?" Then you can elaborate on a style that is harmonious with that of the interviewing organization (why are you there if it isn't?).

Prison or Felony Record

Time spent in prison for a nonfelony can be discovered through gaps in employment by an astute interviewer, or it might just pass. The question on the application is usually asked this way, *"Have you ever been convicted of a felony? If yes, please provide the details."* This gets the matter out in the open as soon as you complete the application. Be ready to provide details. We suggest you jot down the details—dates and final charge(s) of conviction as well as venue.

Be open and honest, but do not offer more information than you are asked for. This is where the application really helps. You can mention it in writing for all to see, and you cannot be accused of hiding information later.

If there was any jail time and it was for an extended period (more than 3 months), there is terminology that may be provided by social workers and career counselors so that you are honest but not sharing more than you need to. Less than 3 months need not be mentioned unless all your time needs to be accounted for elsewhere on the application. Do not lie on the application or during any interviews in the hope the employer will not find out.

Before starting your job search (or even once you've started), take advantage of any public job counselor assistance, such as the Vera Institute of Justice. Additionally, there is always help at the unemployment office, and good career counselors will know employers who have identified themselves as being interested in hiring persons with a felony record. In a tight job market, there are more jobs than people, so it is good because employers may be more willing to accept a felon than in a job market with loads of applicants for each job.

If the question is not asked on the application or during an interview, you are not required to mention it.

Ran Your Own Business; Personal or Business Bankruptcy

9.15 *I see that you were the president of your own company. Why are you looking for a job?*

It had always been my ambition to run my own landscaping firm. I love designing gardens. After 4 years in the business, I found that I spent more time looking for clients, searching for laborers, and dealing with city planners than doing design work. I now have much more appreciation for the entire process, but I would rather invest my future in design work.

I had taken over the business from my partner. Two years after he left, there was one problem after another with suppliers. Shipments were late or damaged. I engaged an attorney to file breach of contract claims; these dragged on through the court system while my bills mounted. Finally, I saw that there was no choice but to file for bankruptcy. In the end, most of the creditors will be fully satisfied; the others have accepted a settlement. All in all, it was quite an education for me.

Serial Absences; Absences Due to Work-Related Illness

If you prepared a functional résumé, this might not come to light, but it may be revealed in an application form or during an interview so it is best dealt with it in advance.

9.16 *I see that there are several long periods of time when you did not work. Why?*

When I tried to move several large boxes into my office, I strained my back. It took several doctors to decide that surgery was needed to repair the damage. I am happy to say that the surgery and follow-up therapy was successful, but I have decided not to move heavy boxes anymore.

I was diagnosed with severe allergies, and it took many days of testing and bad reactions to medications to determine the causes and proper maintenance. For the past 3 years, I have only missed 2 days of work due to illness—it was the flu.

(Note: If the reason for being out of work was due to imprisonment, see "Prison or Felony Record" section above.)

Filed Harassment Claim(s) (or other legal issues pending) against former employer

Any legal proceedings or claims against a former employer should not be discussed nor should an interviewer inquire about them. Refer to the above reasons for leaving. Find the one that has the most truth in it and use it.

Claims Against You

Salary garnishments are actions taken, with the assistance of the federal government, to repay a bad debt. Someone to whom an employee owes a sum of money can go to court to win a judgment. When a court judgment is made, the party who claims that money is owed can then go to the employer to get the employer to reimburse the debt through a payroll deduction. This process is called a garnishment. To raise this question is illegal because federal law protects job applicants from discrimination based on one or more garnishments. If this question is raised, you may say that it is illegal to ask. Beware that this information may be provided as part of a credit report; you usually give to the employer the right to obtain this type of information when you sign the application form without reading the small print just above your signature. (Note: Some employers do a detailed credit check as well as a thorough reference check. If inaccuracies turn up with your answers, your credibility is at risk.)

Special Working Arrangement Needed (Hours or Days)

If there is something that really must be dealt with, wait until the job is offered and you are negotiating terms. If it becomes a deal breaker, then you must make a choice. The same is true for long-range vacation plans or other commitments that affect you. If it is something that is imminent, you can always negotiate a delayed starting date.

9.17 Do you have a problem with overtime?

I have a commitment on Wednesday evenings that I cannot change for the next 8 months. If overtime is required, can I arrange to come in early Wednesday or Thursday morning instead? Any other evening would not be a problem.

9.18 Why did you indicate that you cannot start work for 6 weeks?

I had booked our usual vacation 5 months ago while still at my other job, and I thought that you might prefer not interrupting my start here. If you prefer, I would gladly start immediately and take the time off without pay.

9.19 Are you available to work weekends/evenings/Sundays?

I have a current commitment on _____. If this is a problem, I can reschedule.

If I'm given advance notice, I can work either Saturday or Sunday. Would this be a regular situation?

I can work only on Saturdays due to other commitments.

Note that if you cannot work at any of the times mentioned for religious reasons, you may choose to disclose or not disclose this fact. U.S. Federal law protects those employed by organizations with 15 or more employees who have religious obligations that may detract from employer activities—if the employer can make "reasonable accommodation" to allow the employee to practice his or her faith. Local and state governments frequently have statutes applying to even smaller employers, so check to see what applicable law protects you. Keep in mind that to be protected you need to make your religion known to your employer.

Foreign Worker or Returning Expatriate

Your work experience has not been in the United States because you were employed abroad working for either a foreign or a U.S. organization. The burden is on you to understand the interviewing process as well as the appropriate résumé preparation. Additionally, you must translate your skills and experiences into U.S. terms, selling them to the interviewer and relating them to the needs of the organization. Last, you may have unrealistic expectations of pay scales and job offers. Do extra research into job openings and salary levels for your targeted job.

9.20 *Why do you wish to return to the United States to work now? Why are you seeking work in the United States at this time?*

My personal circumstances have changed.

Or

The political situation has changed.

Or

My company's philosophy has changed, and it will be selling the overseas affiliate.

Or

My career has peaked, and there is no place to go.

I really want to be a part of this exciting economy, I like competition, and I enjoy working. So putting all three together, I decided that this is the place to be.

10
First-Time Job Seeker

Regardless of how far you are along in your career, these are complex times for job hunting. However, things are especially complicated for the first-time job seeker. A lot of misinformation is out there and some odd perceptions as well. Some magazine articles state that, *"current graduates are unprepared . . . poorly educated . . . lacking in practical skills"* while others mention an entry-level college graduate who was offered $200,000. Now it may be true that a recent college grad was offered $200K, but that was no entry-level position! Not all first-time job seekers are recent college graduates nor are they being offered BMWs, enormous salaries, generous relocation expenses, and other perks.

What Type of First-Time Job Seeker Are You?

❏ Never worked before (married right after high school)

❏ Recent graduate of

       High school

       2-year college (associate's degree)

       technical school

       secretarial school

       college (bachelor's degree)

       college (master's degree)

❏ Interrupted your studies to work.

What Is Your Competition?

Basically, you are competing with the same elements that all candidates compete with: looks, youth, brains, brawn, contacts, family, experience, skills, common interests, and pure luck. In addition to all the other first-time job seekers, you are facing off against seasoned workers who are either window shopping or as serious as you are about finding the right job. Like some of them (who have read our books), you are certainly prepared, and you want the job because it is with an organization that you feel passionate about and because the job is a very attractive one.

First-Timer's Preparation

Do your preparation for a job search the same way as everyone else: research, rehearse, and relax. It is how you do the research that may be different. You may have two stumbling blocks in your research: You are

Unsure about what you have to offer.

Uncertain about what is needed.

Luckily the answers are found in more research! Assuming that you have a general goal in mind and some possible jobs targeted, deal with the second uncertainty first—job requirements. Where can you find needed resources?

How about this job? *"Writing, typing, reading, revising, editing, printing, calling, researching, and presenting while alone and unsupervised. No benefits. Endless hours. Unlimited rewards."* This is a description of one of the hardest jobs—finding a job!

The second phase of the research can be more traumatic, and it is not uncommon for job seekers to delay or gloss over it by saying, "I have no skills." If you do not think you have anything to offer, then you will be right. Think instead, "How can I make this happen?"

If you have never worked (as opposed to leaving your career more than a year ago for any reason), what have you been doing? It is really important that you examine your experiences, your skills, and your interests (see Chapter 6, Self-Assessment) to determine what it is that you want to do and can do. In some ways, you may be in a better position than those who 'fell' into jobs or careers and, having spent the past 2, 5, or 10 years in them, are now asking themselves what they want to do—assuming that they raise the issue with themselves at all. The difficult part is finding the value you can add to an organization. You will have to remember what you have done (don't forget any activities, no matter how negligible) and mine them for transferable skills. If you are starting from scratch, there are some questions that you can ask yourself:

❏ Do you prefer working with things, data (information), or people?

❏ What kind of atmosphere do you think you would like: fast-paced, moderate, or slow?

Resources

❏ Classified ads

       Magazines, newspapers, online sources

❏ Counselors

       College, university, community centers

❏ Trade publications

❏ Trade associations

❏ Online job search sites and links to other resources

       Monster.com

       Careers.Yahoo.com

       www.jobtrak.com (for students)

       www.jobweb.org/catapult

       www.CareerMag.com

       www.careers.org

       www.CareerAge.com

       helpwanted2000 (AOL Keyword)

       www.jobseekernews.com

       landjob.com/careers.html

       www.localemployment.com

       (Also search online for "Career resources" and in directories such as About.com for career information)

❏ Networking—meeting with professionals in your chosen field

❑ What kind of hours do you wish to work: 9 to 5, evenings, weekends, compressed workweeks, part time?

❑ Are you willing to travel, either locally or long distances?

❑ Are you planning to take classes in your off hours? Do you have other commitments that you must consider?

❑ Did you ever dream of a specific career? If so, why did you give it up?

❑ Do you have goals now? What will it take to achieve them?

Skills Every Employer Can Use

If you have just graduated from school—any school—you have been engaged in myriad tasks such as time management, research, writing, speaking, possibly working in teams for projects, and learning various subjects. Been home raising a family? When have you used these transferable skills?

Budgeting	Motivating
Coordinating	Organizing
Coordinating projects	Performing public relations
Delegating	Prioritizing
Evaluating	Public speaking
Managing	Teaching

Go back to Chapter 6 and reevaluate on forms called What I Can Do, What I Know, and This Is What I Am Like (another skill!) your entries. Do not neglect the skills you need and are learning while engaged in this job search. These may range from finding out how to research to using the Internet to learning word processing software.

Now you are ready to explain to the interviewer what it is about you that will add value to the job you are being considered for. Try eliminating your competition on those items that you can compete on. Everyone is selling something, but not all candidates are selling the same things. In some ways it is like a chess match—you have to anticipate and counter the other players' moves. What do you think the major hurdles to your candidacy will be?

For example, if you did not have a 4.0 grade point average (or even 3.5), do you have street smarts and practical experience to offer? That is, do you know how to think on your feet, how to thrive under pressure, and how to say the right things by instinct? Do you make a nice presentation? Did you show up on time? Did you come prepared for the interview? Do you have a real passion for the work?

How can you offer something you have (in place of something that they say they want)? A recent graduate, for example, may not have years of experience to offer but does have recent experience with state-of-the-art technology, direct from the classroom under the guidance of an expert. Anyone who has managed a household, including several young children all with the flu, could write volumes on multitasking and prioritizing not to mention epitomizing grace under pressure and working long hours. So, what are your greatest fears? Some can be offset while some cannot; accept it.

Focus on What *You* Can Offer (and What You Want to Offer)

You would be surprised at the number of résumés and marketing letters that omit the essential information: *"This is the job I want."* Once you have done the research and looked at the various skills and experiences that you have accumulated and wish to offer, you have your target(s). You have to do the same homework to prepare for an interview as everyone else does—you are working with a different professional history. The rehearsal and relaxing requirements are also the same.

Regardless of your reasons for not working in the past, concentrate on all the positive reasons you have to work now. Don't say to yourself, *"But, I can't do what I really want." "I need a job, but I do not have many choices." "I have a family to consider."* At times it may seem easier to settle, but you do owe it to yourself to say, *"It looks difficult, but how can I (how can we) make it happen."*

Exploring Alternatives

You may or may not have considered the following:

1. A recruiter or an employment agency
2. Temporary employment
3. Contract or freelance employment

An executive recruiter or an employment agency. The easiest route to finding a recruiter or employment agency is the help-wanted sections of major general circulation newspapers and trade publications as well as

Interview Hurdles	
and how you can leap over them	
I worry that I can't . . .	**But I can . . .**

First Timer's Do's and Don'ts

DO sharpen your skills. Read trade journals; find out what is new, what people are talking about, and what is happening in the job market in your location.

DO talk to people. Network with people who have jobs that you are interested in or in organizations where you would like to work.

DO consider a test drive by taking temporary employment. Get some on-the-job experience while you acquaint (or reacquaint) yourself with the work environment. Try some short-term assignments; one may lead to a full-time job offer.

DO take all interviews. Even it the job does not sound perfect, you need the practice, and going on interviews will help you get over your jitters for the job that you may really want.

DON'T tell your life story. The interviewer is not interested in the exciting details unless they specifically relate to the job.

DON'T limit yourself or be afraid to try something new. Analyze what you did and did not like about your activities so far.

DON'T apologize for taking a hiatus or not working before. Assume that you have been on the right track and you are now ready to begin another phase in your life. This confidence and sense of responsibility will make you valuable in the workplace.

DON'T downgrade poor past experiences gained through volunteering, hobbies, or other interests.

DON'T send mass mailings, generic cover letters, or untargeted résumés.

DON'T assume the interviewer will be willing or able to guess what job you are applying for or are suited for. It is up to you to ask for the job you want (same as everyone else.)

DON'T be unprofessional in behavior or appearance.

online searches. Frequently, the ads refer to the recruiter or agency that is conducting the search. If the recruiter is performing the task on a *contingency basis*, he or she will get paid only if the person placed is placed as a result of his or her efforts. When the hiring arrangement is on a contingency basis, if you have a choice of going directly to the hiring organization or going through the recruiter, by going directly to the organization, you will be giving it the opportunity to fill the position without paying the recruiter (this may be an extra incentive for hiring you).

If the recruiter is being retained to perform the search on a *fee basis*, then regardless of whether he or she makes the placement, the fee will be paid.

If you are a first-time job seeker coming out of a school at the bachelor's degree level or lower (associate's degree, post high school certificate, or even right out of high school), the recruiter will be a contingency firm. If you are graduating from a professional school (for example, if you have just gotten a doctorate in ceramic engineering), it is more likely that the recruiter will be on a retainer basis.

If the recruiter is given a contingency assignment, that is, the recruiter only gets a fee if he or she is responsible for providing the candidate who gets the job offer. It may be very practical and effective to take what may be a mutually beneficial arrangement and that may become the "temp to perm" situation.

Temporary assignments. An employer needs to fill an opening but rather than make the offer outright, the employer agrees to take the person on a temporary basis. Then if the person works out, he or she will be hired as an on-staff employee. While waiting to become a regular employee (which may never happen), the person is working on the employer's premises as a "subcontractor to the employer," and the agency responsible for the placement pays the person. The temp agency is paid from invoices that it sends to the employer. Technically the person performing the tasks is an employee of the agency. These arrangements may or may not include benefits.

The advantage to you of such an arrangement is twofold. First, the employer may be more willing to take a chance than might be true otherwise. The second advantage to you is that you get a chance to show what you can do.

Contract or freelance employment. We know one worker who loves the idea of contract employment. (The contract is between the vendor, who represents you, and the employer, who is getting your services. Often, the arrangement is for a particular project or assignment.) This worker feels that he gets a chance to work for more organizations than he ever otherwise would be able to and that this is an opportunity full of challenges. Each opportunity is a test to see if he can get the organization to offer him a job—which happens with some regularity.

Depending on the area, organizations are taking the "temp to perm" route more and more. If they do it in your area, jump at the opportunity to get your foot (and the rest of you) in the door. If the agency you are talking to doesn't mention it, ask about and see if such an arrangement would be possible for the job(s) you are specifically trying to get.

Often organizations will tell you that the commitment is for 6 weeks or 3 months or "we aren't sure." Frequently, they will add "it may become permanent." If you choose this option, understand that it will keep you from devoting your full-time effort to finding a regular job and that you are somewhat limited in terms of ending the arrangement. Sometimes the agency will give you a contract or letter of agreement. Read the terms of the engagement carefully because they might require you to notify the agency at least 2 weeks in advance of terminating the assignment. If that is what is expected of you, then you should ask for something in writing to say that you will be given 2 weeks' notice of the end of the assignment as well. The reason for this is to practice negotiating and getting you in the habit of reading closely whatever you sign regarding any work arrangement.

Timing

Timing may be more important in some areas than in others. For instance, we know of a graduating liberal arts senior who passed up a first job opportunity with a major software provider for $65,000. She thought that the housing market was so tight where the job was located (in Silicon Valley) that most of her money would go for an apartment. She felt that the East Coast, where she has always lived, would allow her to seek other opportunities without having to move.

Timing also means a lot for a particular skill. About 10 years ago, nurses were in such demand that they were being actively recruited overseas from places as far away as Korea. In such an environment, graduating nurses could pretty much name their price, and benefits grew, so that more flexible working hours and on-site day care became commonplace. Today, programmers and applications developers are in such demand that the situation is reminiscent of the nurse shortage. Just as with the nurse shortage, however, don't be lulled into believing that price is everything.

The employment numbers are favorable toward just about everyone at the time of this writing. Unemployment is at a long-time low throughout the United States and seems to be falling in most places throughout the world. In simple terms, that means that in most places there are a whole lot more jobs than there are employable people to fill them. These macrostatistics can be deceiving. You need to consider what the demand for the job skills are that you are able and willing to provide and compare it to the demand in your area. It may not be helpful to know that 100 miles away there is an acute shortage of employers with your skills if you cannot relocate. Auto workers are in great demand in Michigan where older workers are retiring in ever-greater numbers each year. However, if you are not where those automobile plants are, you may have trouble getting the auto job you want in Brooklyn, New York, despite what the newspaper headlines say about a shortage of auto workers.

Seasonality is another concern you need to address. If you are graduating from college, start interviewing for jobs on campus whenever employers start to visit. If you don't, you will be starting when other graduates, for the most part, are all done. If you are late, however, do not give up. Start your search whenever you can. By taking this approach, you may find opportunities that were not available earlier, or you may find an opportunity because someone who had accepted the position has changed his or her mind.

If you are entering the job market for the first time, remember that any work experience can help your candidacy. Volunteering for short-term projects (helping to staff a charity drive or run an art auction for your children's school) can add points to your candidacy. Seasonal jobs, such as those offered during the summer or during the holiday season, should not be overlooked even though in those times they may be slow to hire full-time workers.

Understand the Interviewer's Agenda

Because you do not have a track record to offer, the burden is on you to link your past experiences (however varied they may be) to the job opening you are interviewing for. You must give the interviewer help in picturing you in the job and working effectively in the organization. The interviewer will buy into your candidacy primarily as a result of your credibility. He or she must believe your statements, since you may not have extensive (recent) proof to support your claims. Additionally, the interviewer may have to stretch his or her imagination to see the relationship between your experiences and what is needed on the job.

Except for your (possible) anxiety and the connections you make between your experience, skills, and personal qualities (those important assessments made in Chapter 6) and the requirements of the job, your interview will proceed as all the others do. Questions raised during the interview may certainly focus on circumstances peculiar to your situation, so preparation along those lines is needed.

Questions

Students

If you are a recent graduate, you will get the usual range of questions about your choices of schools, courses of study, and what other alternatives were available. Additionally, the interviewer may ask questions about your favorite or least favorite subject, teacher or activity; clubs, sports, and student offices you may have held; and any volunteer activities. Answers to these should be basic, straightforward, and honest, slanted as much in your favor as possible and related to the organization and job opening. For example, your interest in the Biology Club (unless you were an officer—for example, treasurer—or were in charge of activities) is not really germane to a job in an accounting firm.

"Why" questions tend to have a negative feel to them; they can come across as an effort to second-guess your choices, even if they are asked as a way for the interviewer to understand you and your thinking. Don't apologize and don't complain!

10.1 Why did you choose that school?

You should have a valid and carefully chosen reason that demonstrates you made your decision after a deliberate thought process. You demonstrate that you are not afraid to make a choice (so you are decisive) but that you gave the subject the attention and time (on-site visits as well as a variety of other research activities) it deserved.

Below are several questions you should be prepared to answer: and be ready to answer in light of your own circumstances.

❑ Where would you have gone to school if you didn't go there?
❑ Why did you switch schools?
❑ What made you choose that major/course of study?
❑ You seem to have changed majors; can you explain why?
❑ Where did you place in your graduating class?

❏ Do you have a transcript? Can we have a transcript?

❏ What extracurricular activities were you engaged in?

❏ What awards or achievements did you receive?

10.2 *You are not planning to go to graduate school? Why?*

I've had enough of school. I am very eager to join the real world and start my career. Frankly, I had a great time during my summer vacations working, and those experiences really whetted my appetite for starting my professional life.

10.3 *Why were your grades so low? What grades did you get in _____ (subject)?*

I am the first to admit that my grades could have been better. I had a choice and that was to be involved in extracurricular, community activities I felt very strongly about.

Yes, my grades could have been better but I paid for a portion of my education by working a part-time job. I also carried a full course load, and my job made it difficult for me to give as much time as I would have liked to my studies. I am proud of the A I got in organic chemistry—one of the toughest, if not the toughest, courses in the entire university.

10.4 *Would your teacher in _____ (subject) recommend you for this position?*

Yes. In fact, he and I had a discussion about job opportunities I should consider, and this was one of the top choices he suggested I look into. Several of his past students were hired here at _____."

10.5 *Why are you interested in talking to us?*

You have developed a truly prestigious organization. You are listed in Fortune's most recent edition of its "The 100 Best Companies To Work For." You also have a great product/service, and you know what to do with the college graduates that you hire.

10.6 *How did you learn of this position?*

I went to the college placement office and saw that your organization was coming. Then I went to your Website to determine what positions you were actively recruiting college graduates for. This was one of ten positions that were posted.

10.7 When could you start?

As soon as you want me.

Graduation is in 2 weeks; I have a few details to take care of, and then I am totally available. I will have completed all the required courses to graduate.

10.8 Explain how your academic training has prepared you to step into this position.

I see that this position requires attention to detail as well as being able to work in a group environment. In my position as a teaching assistant, I helped students with coursework, graded papers, and held weekly study group sessions. Additionally, my courses in _____ required detailed data analysis as well as statistical work. We had several group projects each semester. One project on _____ was very similar to what ABC Company does.

10.9 Did you use a PC (or Mac) in school? What software did you use and for what purposes?

I didn't only use a PC for school; it has become an essential tool in my life. Word processing software has been essential for my term papers, book reviews, and homework assignments. I have used organizer software to manage my time and projects effectively. I use database software for my telephone lists and E-mail addresses and presentation software for overheads and handouts for class presentations. I have even learned to use statistical software that the university makes available for quantitative calculations (for example, regression analysis) that are easily incorporated visually into term papers and overhead presentations. Fortunately the university has really shown the effectiveness of E-mail and the Internet by making them so readily available.

10.10 Tell me about a project or assignment that required you to work with a team.

For our marketing class, we broke up into teams of four and had to build a product and develop a business plan. Two of us on my team were so interested in the product—a scrunchie—that we actually ended up making and selling it locally with some real success. In fact we sold them all. The biggest challenge was getting the other two team members, who took the marketing course only because it was required, to do their share of the work. I personally accepted this problem as a challenge, and I feel I really learned because they both became contributors to the team who carried their own weight.

10.11 Your course of study does not seem to relate to our organization; why are you changing your focus/interviewing with us?

I never felt that college was a trade or vocational school. In fact, when I conducted my research in deciding whether to go to college, I learned that a liberal arts curriculum is really the best preparation for a business career. At the school I attended, the liberal arts program is an intense one that requires every student to conduct thorough research, engage in critical thinking, write in an interesting and comprehensible manner, make frequent classroom presentations, and participate in small group discussions in each of our classes. These are all tools that will make me a successful professional for your organization if you decide to hire me and I decide to accept the offer.

10.12 You need only _____credits to get your certificate/ diploma. Why are you not continuing with your studies?

As soon as I establish a work schedule, I will register for either weekend and evening classes or distance learning. I plan to complete my studies and get my diploma in _____. Also, I feel that working while I complete my coursework will make the learning more practical and immediate.

10.13 Why did it take you so long, ___ years, to complete your studies?

The only way I could go to college was to pay my own way. I had to work 40-hour weeks, and felt I would be able to complete only _____ courses per semester. I am proud that I did it and proud it did not take me longer and proud that my GPA ended up at _____.

10.14 Why didn't you take any summer jobs/part-time jobs while you were in school?

I had terrific opportunities in the summers to go to _____ and/or study _____.

Or

I was so burned out from the intensity of the academic program and my extracurricular activities that I used the summers to recharge my battery.

Because of commitments to _____ I would have only been available to work _____ (amount of time), and I thought I would not even be considered.

Or

The only jobs available were for lifeguards, and I felt it would not be the optimum use of my time, so I did some independent study instead.

(Be prepared to discuss your independent study program.)

Or

I had been thinking of joining Habitat for Humanity but realized that it would be an additional expense for my family. So rather than do that, I stayed home, but by the time I made that decision it was too late to find summer employment so I took baby/house sitting, lawn mowing/construction work instead.

10.15   Why didn't you have any internships?

My program did not allow it.

I could not afford it.

10.16   Have you dropped out of school? Why have you dropped out of school?

When I graduated from high school, there seemed to be no choice besides college. And there was only one college I could attend. Going was a big mistake for me. I really wanted to spend some time in the world, figuring out what I wanted to do with the rest of my life. I tried college but realized it was the wrong time so I dropped out.

Or

I started college and loved it, but then my family ran into difficulty and I felt my first obligation was to them, so I dropped out of school to help out.

10.17   Do you feel your grades are an indication of your academic achievement?

You need to make the point that the key person in any personal evaluation is the person him or herself. There is no need to cry about poor grades or boast about great ones.

Yes and no. The higher up you go on the academic ladder, the more subjective the ratings become. I did quite well gradewise, but I wonder if the results I obtained were an accurate barometer of what I learned. Regardless of grades, the ultimate determinant is me. The same is true for my career and the results I get there.

10.18   Describe your most rewarding college/business experience.

Cite a situation in which you were really challenged and you succeeded.

Being selected chairperson of the Winter Carnival was my first opportunity to really build a project of big magnitude (we had a $1 million budget) from scratch. I found it truly memorable to build the program and the team and then watch all the pieces come together. The fact that we were able to provide a return of $55,000 to the university was personally very satisfying as well.

10.19 Describe a situation in which you needed to involve others in order to perform a task. What part did you play, and what was the outcome?

In this question the interviewer is attempting to determine how you work as part of a team. Be careful to say "we" and not "I" when describing a situation.

> *I really wanted to be class president, but I did not want to appear self-serving, so when candidates were being considered I was careful to ask a few close friends who were active in the nomination committee what they thought about my running for president. They told me they had thought of me, but they thought I would not be interested. Once I assured them I was, they were active participants in securing my nomination. During the campaign, they were tireless and on election day I won by a very narrow margin. I will always remember that I never would have even been nominated without their encouragement and support. It was a memorable and humbling experience. I really learned the importance of getting things done through others.*

Never Worked

Depending on how old you look (and interviewers may not ask your age), your age can be more or less important. Additionally, the reasons you give for deciding to work now and what you have done with your time previously will also be taken into consideration. If the reasons made sense to you at the time, they will probably make sense to the interviewer. In any case, that was then, and this is now.

10.20 I see that you have never been employed. Would you please explain this?

> *Right after high school I got married and shortly thereafter began to raise a family. We felt that my being a full-time mom was a full-time job.*
>
> *Right after high school I got married, and we adopted a child. Given the circumstances at the time (my spouse was in the service), I opted to be a full-time parent.*
>
> *After graduation, my grandparents invited me to stay with them in Italy. They were elderly, and I stayed on for two and a half years. Three months ago they came to live with my parents here in the United States.*

10.21 Are you willing to spend 6/9/12 months as a trainee?

A great answer here will be a strong sell.

I really want to start a career with this organization and stay for the long haul. If you feel that a training period will make me a more effective employee and you are willing to make the investment, then I will certainly put in the time. I have always proven to be a fast learner, and I am certainly motivated because I want to succeed here.

10.22   You have said you want to start your career with us. Define "career" as it pertains to you.

A career is a series of progressive steps that allow one to grow professionally by stretching the person each step of the way. A great career is one in which an individual never stops learning and grows by taking increasing responsibility while being overseen by those who know what she or he needs to know in order to be effective and successful.

10.23   Looking at your résumé, I see that you volunteered at _____. Could you tell me about your experiences there?

I worked in the office planning the event for nearly 5 months. I was involved in everything because we were such a small group. I designed and ordered brochures and T-shirts; I signed up and kept track of volunteers. Working with a planning team, we arranged all the facilities needed for the event from donations of water bottles to balloons. In the end, we raised 12 percent more in funds over the prior year, and we all had a great time doing it.

10.24   You mentioned that you have experience with _____. When was the last time you used that technical program?

I learned to use that software doing our family's checkbooks on our own computer. Eventually, I also kept track of all our investments, loans, and mortgages. When we were offered the option to pay our bills online, I leapt at the opportunity to save more time. It has proven to be very efficient although, after research, I changed over to _____, an even better program.

10.25   Why should we hire you instead of someone more experienced/more qualified?

Even though I have not had a traditional work history, I have never been idle. Whether I am learning new programs on our home Mac or volunteering in the library or dealing with the contractors when we remodeled our kitchen, I am constantly organizing and monitoring, and I am very efficient. When time is at a premium, you learn to do a lot quickly. I am excited to have time now for full-time work. As a result of working with many different parents over the years on class projects, I have learned to be effective will all types of people. I think I have a high energy level to offer and have proven to be a quick learner. For years I have been a customer at _____, and the prospect of selling the merchandise that I know so well is exciting.

10.26 *Why do you wish to work part-time/on a temporary basis/as a freelancer?*

Eventually, I would like to work full time, but, for now, a part-time position would make maximum use of my available time while allowing me to continue to meet my other obligations.

I think I would really enjoy working in different organizations; in school, I interacted with all levels of students and faculty effectively. I have skills that can be used by many different types of businesses, and I have the transportation that would allow me to take assignments in a variety of locations. Both the companies I work for and I would benefit from this arrangement.

Actually, depending on what hours are available on a part-time basis, I plan to register for classes at _____ to continue my studies.

10.27 *Describe how you set priorities.*

Here take advantage of your recent school experience (if this is your situation) to illustrate the skills you developed that can now be applied to work.

At school I always had to update priorities based on the most recent information available regarding a project, homework assignment, or scheduled test(s). Once I have the new information, I have always been effective at planning how the new requirements will alter the approach I am taking to complete all the assignments. With the help of my PC and a good organizer program, I reset targets and dates using a "chunking system"—that is, break down each project into significant "chunks" and then proceed to knock them down one at a time.

10.28 *What are the most important rewards you expect to receive in your career?*

This answer should be an easy one because you should be giving it ongoing attention as you consider career options and opportunities.

One is the reward of knowing that there are continuing challenges in the job that you have.

. . . the opportunity to grow professionally.

. . . to work for an organization that is responsible for a product or service of which I am proud.

. . . to work for an organization that realizes what separates it from all other organizations is the talented group of individuals that comprise its staff. I

understand your organization feels that it is only by attracting the most talented people and nurturing them with ongoing training and professional development that will allow the organization to compete successfully and be as effective as it is.

10.29 What are your career objectives? How do you plan to achieve your career objectives?

This is a question that should never go away.

I have really developed an interest in TV production while taking TV courses in college. To challenge that interest and to determine whether that is a career I want to pursue, I applied for TV internships and was fortunate to get three different ones. Now I would like to get an entry-level job as a production assistant for a major TV company so that I can pursue my ultimate goal of becoming a producer.

Brief, to the point, and obviously well thought out.

10.30 What are your plans for continuing your education?

This is a valid and obvious question for any first-time job seeker. The interviewer is genuinely interested in your career path and wonders, rightfully so, if you have any plans to continue school in the near or distant future. The only negative response is the direct *"I have no plans to continue right now. I have really had enough of school. It was great while it lasted, but it is time to move on."* There is no reason to say, *"I will put off a decision for graduate school to a later date."* To reinforce the point, what this statement tagged onto the end says is that you are really thinking about grad school somewhere down the line. There is no reason to plant that seed in the interviewer's mind.

11
Out Of the Loop
Unemployed for More than 1 Year

Whether you planned it or not, you have not been employed for over 1 year, and your situation will have to be explained in an interview. How did you get into this position, and what have you been doing about it?

You may have taken a job in the interim, and it just did not work out. You may have done some freelance or part-time work when something came your way. Or you may have vegged out and now know the story line of every soap opera on television. Maybe you put your time to good use: learned some new skills, taken some classes, or at least watched television interviews for some insights into proper interviewing techniques (not the ones where the guests yell and fight with each other, please!).

Or maybe you have been looking for a job actively and have not found the job you want. Have you even been given the chance to turn down a job? (If you are totally clueless and have no idea how to conduct a job search, you need a more comprehensive approach; consider our other publication, *Get a Job in 30 Days or Less*.)

Choice or Chance?

Have you been looking and been unable to find:

❑ A job you like?

❑ Any job?

Have you been looking at all? Conducting a minimal job search? Or have you really been looking but to no avail?

Job Search History

Date: _____

Last Employer: _____

    Dates: From: _____ to _____

Reason for leaving: _____

_____

Job sought: _____

Where have you looked? _____

· ·

Job offers (details): from _____

Position: _____ Salary: _____

Why not accepted: _____

Job offers (details): from _____

Position: _____ Salary: _____

Why not accepted: _____

Current status (interviews scheduled):

    Employer: _____

    Position: _____

Target: _____

_____

First, what is the reason that you are looking for a job at this time? Were you downsized, let go, laid off, fired, or allowed to resign? Did you choose to leave thinking you had another job but it did not work out? Did you relocate and were surprised at the tight job market in your new location? Did you get overly annoyed with someone at work and summarily quit?

Second, why do you feel that you have not found a job since leaving your last employer? Exactly what type of job have you been searching for? Where have you looked? What methods have you employed (classified ads, referrals, online resources, or recruiters)? Where have you put in the most time? If your search has not gotten the desired results (job offers), it is important that you know why. No job offers after months of looking can mean either that you are looking in the wrong places or that you are looking for the wrong job: both situations are correctable.

Are you returning to the job market? Most people returning to the job market are usually homemakers who wish to work once their children are grown. However, there are many other valid reasons for returning to work, including financial necessity. If you have been home ostensibly writing the great American novel and have suddenly tired of a life in fiction, then you are in this category. It is not so much why you were not working, but why you want to work now that is important. Also of prime importance is what you have to offer to a prospective employer in an interview. Some explanations for leaving the workforce for an extended period of time are simple: *"I went back to school." "I raised a family." "I tried to run my own business." "I needed to take time off for an ill relative."*

Singing the "Turned Down" Blues?

What do you think the real reason is that you have not found a job if you have been looking actively? What do interviewers say is the reason that you have not been offered a job? Are you getting interviews?

Take a moment now to review your résumé and copies of the marketing letters you sent out. The problem could be right in front of your eyes! If you have been actively looking for a job to no avail and have been going on interviews, what were the reasons that you were given for not being hired?

"No openings at this time."

"Not what we are looking for."

"Hired someone with better credentials/better skills/more experience."

"We decided to hire from within."

"You were our second choice . . ."

"We are not filling the position."

No response at all.

There is a song with the lyrics, *"If you want to be somebody else, change your mind."* If you are trying to be somebody else, change your ways! If interviewers are saying, *"You were this close . . . ,"* persevere; you are on the right track. If interviewers tell you that they went with someone with better skills or more experience, they are telling you something that you should hear. Either you are targeting the wrong jobs or overvaluing your own skills.

Does this sound familiar? *"I feel like I have been on a hundred interviews and have not gotten one job offer. I am getting depressed. I really need a job now . . . . I will take anything offered!"* If this is how you feel, you are probably telegraphing your desperation to every interviewer you come across. No organization (and no recruiter) wants to be "any port in a storm."

Try this:

1. What are the reasons you are being given for not being hired? Is there a trend? Are you talking yourself out of the jobs? How are the interviews themselves—are you connecting with the interviewer? Obviously, there was something in your résumé that made the organization feel you are a possible hire. Why did this change after the interviewer saw you in person?

2. Examine your résumé and marketing letter; are they specifically targeted for the jobs and organizations you are looking at? Or are they just copied and sent to "Dear Sir or Madam"?

3. Look again at jobs you are aiming at: do you have the right and current skills needed? Do you need to aim higher or lower or in another area entirely?

4. Is there a skeleton in your closet you don't know about? If employers are checking references, is one coming up poorly? Is your credit rating revealing your fiscal faults? If you are a recent graduate, your schools may be called to verify your graduation date as well as the type of certificate or diploma you received. Were you honest about this information?

5. Do the reactions you get seem totally unreasonable? You have had job offers (or near offers) dissolve and you have no idea why. Do you know what is being discovered about you in a background check? The information may be incorrect or not even yours! Even though this is not a widespread problem, it can and does happen. A few incorrect keystrokes by a data entry clerk and your credit history could be changed from glowing to deadbeat. It only costs about $40 to do a background check on yourself; use any search engine to look for "background check." Then find one and do one for your peace of mind. (For stories on stolen identities see msnbc.com; search for "stolen identity" in the database.)

6. Assuming that you have made a credible presentation at the interviews and no other solutions come to mind, seek out a career counselor at the

unemployment office, your local community center, or your school career development office.

Assuming that you are targeting jobs that are probable and are just beginning your job search after an extensive hiatus, you literally have to get back into the loop. You have to account for the intervening time, explain why you are looking now, and match yourself to the job opening and the organization. You are competing with all those other candidates who have not been out of the workforce so you will have to sell your reasoning to an interviewer. You will have to show that you are up to date, energetic, and interested in the position in addition to being qualified.

What Have You Been Doing in the Meantime?

If you have not been part of the active workforce for over 1 year (for whatever reason), what have you done in the interim to keep your skills current, remain up to date with your industry and profession, and gain marketable experience?

Self-assessment is extremely important because you may have to look harder for transferable skills. Try thinking backwards: consider all of the skills and personal qualities needed to perform the job that you are interested in. Then think about every activity that you have been involved in— which skills did you use and what skills did you learn recently? Do not ignore volunteer work, charity or religious activities, and classes that you may have taken. Complete the assessment forms in Chapter 6 if you have not already done so. (If it has really been a long time since you worked (over 5 years), refer to Chapter 10 for additional advice.)

Why are you reentering the job market at this particular time? Regardless of your reason for not working, you will be asked the reason why you are returning to work. Financial reasons are not what the employer is interested in. He or she will want to know why you want to work for that particular organization doing that particular job and why you think you can do it (better than other applicants). You first have to answer these questions for yourself before you can credibly respond to them in an interview.

Additionally, the interviewer will probably ask about other job offers you may have received and where else you have looked. This information can be briefly shared in the spirit of reciprocity and disclosure.

Interim Audit		
Date of last employment: _____		
Account for your activities in intervening months and cite any experience or skills that relate to your job search. Include any short-term or consulting jobs.		
Dates	**Details of Activities**	**Related Skills and Experience**

Psyching Yourself Up

Reevaluate your job goals and career path by asking yourself the following questions:

❑ What job are you looking for and why?

❑ How long have you been looking?

❑ How much time and effort have you put into your search?

❑ What did you start looking for over 1 year ago, and what are you looking for now? Has your goal changed? If so, why?

❑ If you are seeking to return to the workforce, what was your prior profession and what are you looking for now?

❑ If your goals are different, why are they different?

The answers to these questions may seem obvious to you, but it is quite another matter to verbalize them and respond to the questions credibly in an interview. Understanding your reasons is different from explaining them. Knowing where you are now and how you got to this point is one aspect of your self-evaluation; the next step is knowing where you want to go.

Long-Range Goals

An interviewer might expect that the time you spent away from employment may have involved some thinking and soul-searching on your part. You may have reevaluated what you want from a job and employer as well as what you have to offer. Look forward and determine what your goals are for the next 5 or 10 years. How do you plan to achieve these goals? How do your current goals differ from the goals you had 5 or 10 years ago? Why have your goals changed? How have you changed?

There are many self-help books and talk show discussions about "following your dream" that make it seem that it is only the matter of your perseverance. Granted that a lot of determination and effort go into someone finally realizing a long-sought-after dream. However, there must be some practicality and realism to the dream. Wanting to be an Olympic swimmer at age 40 may be a terrific ambition but even with the ability and access to water, it may be unrealistic. Even with a more realistic dream, you will need opportunity and financial means. It seems like a favorite subject of news stories is about the financially secure, successful business executive that quits his or her job and goes off to follow the dream of a lifetime—studying cacti in the Mojave Desert! If you do have a dream—a career change or a new job—what are the steps you will need to take to attain it? Since you are reentering the workforce, it is well worth your time to assess the direction you will take. Are you just looking for a decent job at a fair rate or is there something else on your agenda?

Problems from the Employer's Viewpoint

Depending on your reasons for unemployment, an interviewer might think that you are a "little slow out of the gate" professionally, having missed work time being unemployed. If you can demonstrate that you have not only considered this interview but also where you want to go professionally, you will evidence a professional and businesslike attitude.

Interviewers may wonder about or ask you:

- ❑ *Are your skills dusty, out of date?*
- ❑ *Is this an energetic, "with it" potential employee?*
- ❑ *If no one else wanted to hire you, why should I?*
- ❑ *What is the* real *problem with this candidate?*
- ❑ *How long will you last here? Will you want to return to a life of leisure?*
- ❑ *Do you understand today's workplace and economy?*

List all your self-doubts and concerns—the interviewer will probably have the same ones and more besides. The way to win the interviewer over is with credible, well-thought-out answers.

Could this be you? *"It has been years since I worked and even longer since I interviewed. I am a nervous wreck about the first interview. What can I do?"* Regardless of what you read, you will be nervous, so accept it. You are nervous because this is new and you are uncertain about your ability to hold your own in an interview. If you can, make your first interview be for a job that you are not all that excited about. It may be a little too far to travel; it may offer a pay scale that is less than you want. Take it as practice. As we have said in other chapters, practice will improve your techniques. Ask someone who is in the field (a former coworker) to put you through your paces in a practice interview. Each interview will get easier, and you will be less nervous. Every performer gets a certain amount of performance anxiety; use the adrenaline to your advantage!

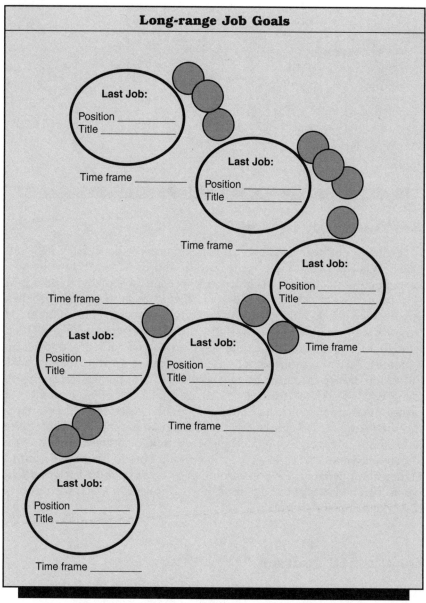

Long-range Job Goals

Last Job:

Position _____
Title _____

Time frame _____

Last Job:

Position _____
Title _____

Time frame _____

Last Job:

Position _____
Title _____

Time frame _____

Time frame _____

Last Job:

Position _____
Title _____

Last Job:

Position _____
Title _____

Time frame _____

Last Job:

Position _____
Title _____

Time frame _____

Keeping Up Professionally
❏ Professional associations or organizations
❏ Workshops or seminars
❏ Courses—traditional or online
❏ Mentors, business associates
❏ Journals, trade papers, magazines
❏ Self-study: _____
❏ Other _____

Are You Ready to Work?

If you have not been active in your field recently, how dusty are your skills? What are you doing right now to improve them? How are you keeping current? If you are slightly red-faced and sheepishly thinking, *"It is all I have to do to look for a job; now you want me to do other stuff too?"* then you do need a kick in the rear! While you were looking, your competition was working and learning new skills. If your embarrassment has faded enough for you to take action, plan right now what you will do to get up to date and keep up professionally. Activities can range from taking books out of the library to learning a new skill (speaking French for example), using a CD-ROM to learning HTML to make Websites, or joining a professional organization and attending regular meetings. Other options include taking formal classes, volunteering, or attending workshops. Not all of these involve great commitments of time or money. How do you know you want to work in a particular field if you do not have the information about what is going on currently? If you are coming back to a field where you had worked at one time, have you kept in touch with former coworkers and supervisors?

How to Sell Yourself

If you have not been interviewed in a while, double-check your interview preparation and dress. Have you done the research into your prospective employer(s) and yourself? It is so easy to skip this back-office work, but despite a tight job market (as of January 2001), employers still seek to hire the best, and there are a lot of "perennials" out there, always looking for a job—even if they already have one. It is a crowded job market with a proliferation of résumés just generating more work for the harried interviewer or recruiter.

Here are some rules to follow for selling yourself in your situation:

❏ Believe that you are a terrific candidate and that you will make a great hire.

❏ Look and act as if you already work for the organization.

❏ Be professional and courteous.

❏ Listen.

❏ Do a show-and-tell: what value can you add to the employer?

❏ Use your insight into what the employer is looking for and needs in order to promote your candidacy.

❏ Want the job and ask for it.

The two areas where you may need a little boosting is in the confidence department and being certain that you are targeting the right jobs. Review the skill matching exercise and assessment worksheets in Chapter 6. Are you certain you are on the right track? Is your job target both possible and probable? Are you being realistic? You may fit the educational and physical requirements for an astronaut, but, since so few are hired, is it probable that you will get hired? Interested in the agribusiness field? Perhaps New York City is not the best place to look.

The more information that you have about yourself, the current job market, and possible employers, then the more confident that you will feel. Uncertainty tends to breed insecurity.

If you could do the last interview over, what would you have done differently? Starting right now, keep a log or journal for all your interviews. Take notes on whom you saw, research done for the job opening, what was discussed, and your opinion of the interview and organization. You can use these notes if you get called back for a second interview as well for self-review of your performance and the interviewer's.

Is there any particular area of your background that makes you feel nervous or insecure about discussing in an interview? Have you ever asked an interviewer for feedback, such as:

"Are there any suggestions you could make about my interview or job search?"

"Would you consider me for other openings as they occur?"

"Is there any particular reason why I was not selected for the job?"

Do you match your résumé? Are you both in the same "voice"? A bouncy, creative résumé and cover letter should produce a bouncy, creative interviewee. Do not use language in your cover letter that does not paint a picture of who you are—you may shock or disappoint the interviewer.

Interview Log

After every interview write down the details.

Date:_____ Organization: _____

Interviewer: _____ Title/Dept.: _____

Job opening: _____

How learned of opening/referred by: _____

Research: _____

Main points of interview: _____

_____

Did you cover your agenda? _____

_____

Comments on interview/organization/job: _____

_____

_____

Your weakest points: _____

Your strongest points: _____

Next step(s): _____

_____

Thank-you letter sent: _____ Do you want the job?: _____

Why/why not? _____

Follow-up/status): _____

Questions

11.1   *What is the reason you are seeking work now?*

This is an obvious subject to explore. If you have personal reasons for having to return to the workforce (debts to pay, an ill spouse to support, or just sheer boredom from being at home) these are not reasons to share in an interview. They all speak of going away from something—you should sell yourself as actively going forward in your career.

I left my last position to care for an ailing family member. Recently he passed away, and I am now available for full-time work. I was glad I was able to repay his kindness to me, and I am very excited to be able to continue my career in _____. I have managed to attend trade shows and have kept up with current events, both online and in other media.

For the past ____ years I was content to take care of my family. For some time now I have considered returning to the workforce, utilizing my skills and experience in _____. ABC Company appears to be a growing, dynamic company that can use my energy and experience. I have never lost my interest in _____ and am excited at the opportunity to use my skills here at _____.

11.2   *What were you doing while you were not working? How have you kept yourself occupied?*

Stick to business-related endeavors; no one is interested in how you improved your tennis score or how fast you can win at solitaire. Refer to what you wrote in the Interim Audit you completed earlier in this chapter.

11.3   *How did you prepare for this interview? How did you research our organization?*

Even though I was experienced in finding a job in the past, I realized that there might be some new tricks I could learn. The one trick I took advantage of was doing research for jobs and organizations online. There is a wealth of information available, a lot of it on your Website. I also spoke with others in the field as to what companies they could recommend. Mr. ____ of _____ spoke very highly of your organization, and I looked further into it, finding the job opening on your Website.

11.4   *Why would you consider a cut in pay to take this job?*

I am so impressed with this organization and the career opportunity that I am willing to do what it takes to get this job.

Or

If you are comparing base to base, it is a pay cut. But I have looked carefully at the total compensation and benefits package and the combination of an early job review, a lower pay deduction for medical benefits, and the closer location all add up to at least a lateral move for me right now. Down the road I am hoping I will quickly get back to where I was and then some.

11.5 Why would you want to move to this city/part of the country?

If you have friends or relatives in the area, say so. If you have visited the area for business or vacation, mention it briefly.

Believe it or not, it is attractive to me. I have done some research and discussed it with my family. Considering our lifestyle, there are advantages to moving to this area that include _____. The fact is that your organization and the position we are discussing are so attractive that moving to this area is worth considering because of the career opportunity.

11.6 I see that you have not worked for nearly 4 years. Why was this?

I am glad that you raised this issue. The fact is I have been in prison because I was convicted of a crime. The crime was a nonviolent one, and I learned from my mistake. I have paid my debt to society, and now I am ready to provide for my family and myself. This job is something I really am ready to do and do well. Give me the opportunity, and I will not disappoint you.

I had a plan to start my own business. I found a partner. We put together seed money, signed a lease, and opened. At first it was really exciting putting in the long hours and identifying revenue opportunities. As time passed though we realized that we were burning out, and the real earnings that we had hoped for went back into the business. Just recently, we closed our doors/sold the business. Having done it, I am ready to become an employee again. To me, it is more exciting to be a part of a large group that brings a variety of specializations to the table than trying at all times to wear many and various hats.

11.7 What have you done that shows initiative and your willingness to work?

From the days of my first newspaper route/lemonade stand/lawn mowing job I have always wanted to work and loved working. Most recently when my occupation was falling into decline and obsolescence, I took whatever I could get just to work. Now through diligence and persistence I have found another career and in the short time I have been a _____ I think you will agree that I have progressed very quickly.

11.8 What have you done to continue your personal development?

I have engaged in a variety of activities. Let me share a few with you. For starters, I begin each day by scanning the papers to see what is new and what happened yesterday. Then I go on the Net for about a half an hour and visit my favorite Websites to see what is going on in my field. Once a week I make it a practice to meet for lunch or a cup of coffee with a professional colleague or attend a meeting with other professionals.

11.9 What did you tell your last employer when you said that you wanted to leave their employ after only a few months there?

I explained that . . .

. . . the job was explained to me initially very differently; I had hoped that it would evolve into a job that was closer to that which I thought it would be but I could see that would not be the case.

. . . the organization seems to be changing its focus and my ability to make a positive contribution to its goals seems too stifled. I would prefer to work where I could make a difference.

. . . the new management that has recently come onboard is bringing in their own staff; I would rather start my new job search now.

It was 7 months into my job search when I was hired by _____. I admit I jumped into this job hastily, not considering what I really wanted. Two weeks later I realized I had made a serious mistake. Even though I had misgivings, I committed myself to making the job work. My word is important to me, and I do not renege on my obligations. After 3 months, both the supervisor and I agreed that I had tried but this was not the job for me. I resigned when he had a replacement, and I am back looking again, but wiser for the experience.

11.10 What personal, non-job-related goals have you set for yourself?

To take the time—regardless of how busy I may be at work—to engage in activity that will recharge my battery so that I will be energized when I return to work. My activities range from spending time with my family to reading a serious book or taking a jog.

11.11 When was the last time you doubted your professional abilities?

I have never doubted my professional abilities. In fact, the more I am engaged in my profession, the more I see that what I have learned through experience really cannot be obtained in books or a classroom. Let me tell you, though, that I have doubted the long-term survival of my profession on occasion. Technology shifts and management changes occasionally in the past have made it seem as if there is little regard for my profession, and I wondered if it would have much of a role in the future. Right now though I see a resurgence, and these demanding times require professionals who really understand the big picture. You can get that only with a variety of experiences in a broad range of settings over a period of years.

11.12 Your education seems dated. Are you taking any classes now?

At this time I am not, but I am considering a course of study that emphasizes _____. What I need to do first however is get a job and then see what demands on my time the job makes. At that point I will be able to assess whether I will take the course I am considering. The time has to be right, and my first priority is to my employer and the position I am in.

11.13 What have you learned from your past jobs?

A variety of things. First I have learned the importance of dealing with people and the balance one must place between considering people's feelings and getting things done. I have also learned the importance of communication—especially on the upward side. You can never overcommunicate with your boss. A third thing I've learned is to never overpromise; if anything, overdeliver.

11.14 What have you learned from your past mistakes?

If something is worth doing, it is worth doing well. If you need help, ask for it as soon as you realize it, not when it is too late. If you are wrong, admit it. Make sure you do appropriate research before you join an organization.

11.15 What is the biggest change you have made in your life in the past 5/10/15 years?

The biggest change of the past 15 years has been the connection I have made to the personal computer and other forms of technology which enable me to work more effectively.

Learning to deal with a more diverse population. Hiring has expanded, and the need for good people has not been satisfied. When I first started, I worked with people very much like me in background at _____. In the past 5 or 6 years, I have seen great changes. I am meeting and working with people I never would have come in contact with before, and it is amazing. It is exciting to see that despite some cultural or language differences, we are all pretty much the same, trying to provide a better life for our families.

11.16 What kinds of new technology do you use? What do you use it for?

For starters, I use the PC and the Internet. Word processing, accounting, presentation, database, and E-mail/organizer software have all made it possible for me to concentrate on analysis instead of spending all my time compiling data.

11.17 What have you read recently in your field/or about _____?

Always be ready with two or three recent books that are highly regarded and not considered merely superficial works related to your field.

11.18 Do you have any favorite bookmarks?

If you do not understand this question, you have labeled yourself Internet-impaired. Bookmarks are how favorite Websites are "remembered" by your computer browser. As with questions about reading material, movies, television or Websites, relate your choices to the job at hand.

11.19 Where else have you looked? How long have you been actively looking?

I have been looking on and off for a while, but only recently did I decide to really focus on finding a job. I have been looking exclusively in fashion. In fact I have been back to two/a few companies, and it looks like they are both close to making me an offer.

11.20 Have you received any job offers?

A few of the jobs I interviewed for turned out to be very different than advertised. I recently was invited back for a second interview with a department head that could be a real possibility. Since I have just started my search, I am not overly concerned.

11.21 Why were you out of work for a year?

If your résumé shows no regular, long-term employer for the past year, you can expect this kind of question. However, being out of work is not the same as taking temporary work, so do not confuse the two. They are not synonymous in the eye of your interviewer. If he or she is confused, address it directly and briefly.

There seems to be a misunderstanding. I have not been out of work for a year. As my résumé states, I have been taking temporary jobs for the past year. I really enjoyed it.

12
You Need a Story

Your work history may not be as straightforward and traditional as employers might expect; it may not even be what you wish to dwell on in an interview.

- ❏ You may have made a few 'not so great' decisions.
- ❏ You may have gaps in your employment.
- ❏ Your work history may have a few twists and turns in it.
- ❏ You may have left a former employer under less than ideal circumstances: for example, you may have been fired; you quit because of personal differences with management; you just decided to not show up for work; or you left because of family or personal obligations.

These issues may be revealed in your résumé, may come up when you fill out a job application, or will be discovered during the interview. You need to explain yourself; you need a story to relate. (We do not mean fiction—we mean a planned, concise explanation.)

Understanding Your Decision(s)

Why are you here now? How did you arrive at this point in your career? Was it because of those twists and turns in your employment history or despite them?

Review the Professional History you completed in Chapter 6. Think about why you took each job and why you left each job. It may be easy to justify your decisions based on the circumstances at the time; others may be inexplicable, even to you. Some jobs just ended (summer jobs, projects), while others were outgrown (better opportunities elsewhere, promotions, or greater compensation). This is not just another idle exercise; often you are asked questions in an interview about your reasons for taking and leaving jobs. You are frequently asked to explain events in your personal history. Another question that may come up is, To what degree have you planned your professional life or did it just happen?

One of the points we make repeatedly in all our career books is that searching for a job is work in of itself but it should be an enjoyable, exciting process. Many times it is the homework—the planning, the preparation, the introspection, and the self-analysis—that the job seeker gives short shrift to. Having most of the answers for your own sake in advance will take much of the anxiety out of interviewing. Who knows what you will discover about yourself in the process?

Situation: My spouse is in the military, and we had to relocate several times. How can I get an employer to hire me, not knowing how long I will be able to stay?

Before attempting to address this issue, break it down into specifics. Refer to the Work History you just completed. Try to determine whether there is a pattern to the amount of time you stayed in one place. In the worst-case scenario, if the tours of duty are extremely short (that is, 6 months or less), then the best option to consider is a temp job or seasonal work. The best-case scenario is two or more years in one place. In this event, most employers would be glad to get 2 years of employment from a new employee. Furthermore, are any of the companies where you previously worked located in your current location? If so, go back to your past sources in the organization and determine whether they would like to reemploy you. Finally, consider project work. Check the papers and local Websites (search locally for freelance or contract employees) to see if there is a demand for workers to meet a specific need that will be only temporary.

Now that you have examined and you understand your reasons for past actions and decisions, you have to explain and sell them. You have to link these actions and decisions to skills, qualities, and talents that are attractive to a prospective employer. Do they make good business sense? What do they say about your decision-making abilities and your priorities? One of the best aspects of this retrospective is knowing that everyone learns and changes along the way; no matter what has happened in the past, it can be different now if you wish to make the effort. What are you doing now that is different?

Understanding Your Work History

List below your past jobs, with the most recent first. Next to each, write why you took each job (what you liked about it) and why you left (what you disliked/reasons).

Job: _____ Dates _____

    Why taken: _____

_____

    Why left: _____

_____

Job: _____ Dates _____

    Why taken: _____

_____

    Why left: _____

_____

Job: _____ Dates _____

    Why taken: _____

_____

    Why left: _____

_____

Situation: I think my former employers may be giving me poor references, effectively blackballing me. They were miserable to work for, which was why I quit. How can I check into this? Deal with this?

There are several ways to deal with this situation.

1. Ask your former employer what is being given out when asked for a reference. Do this in a nonconfrontational manner. Determine what is the company policy on references.

2. Seek help from former colleagues and supervisors. Be frank with them and ask that they be the same. A lukewarm reference can "damn you with faint praise." Ask for their approval to give their name out as a reference.

3. Consider doing an investigation. As we discussed on page 178 (#s 4 and 5) find out what previous employer(s) are saying about you.

Making Changes

Are you looking for

The same job—different industry?

A different job—same industry?

A different job—different industry?

In each case, you must draw parallels or create links with your prior history and your potential new career. Keep in mind the three things the employer is looking for: can do, will do, and fit. Make a case for each of these categories in your interview.

For example, a secretary working in a construction company wishes to take a job in an architecture firm. What are the duties of a secretary that would probably be the same in each? These are the transferable skills to stress, the "can do" element. Research into the specific duties of a secretary in an architectural firm reveals that keeping track of projects, scheduling meetings with clients and vendors, and typing reports are activities that are comparable to those you had in prior jobs. Having to deal with government agencies and checking on a variety of licenses will require making new contacts and learning new procedures, but you had some limited involvement in similar tasks at the construction company. A strong work record combined with an affable nature and genuine interest in the industry are also pluses to stress; efforts to research the industry show eagerness and willingness to learn. All elements add "will do" and "fit."

A complete change of both job and industry requires more research into the requirements for the new position and the new industry as well as finding transferable skills. Another issue that needs explaining is why you want to make such a change. Usually, if it is a well-thought-out decision, the reasons that are good enough for you are also good enough for an interviewer.

Positive Reasons for Change
Or what the interviewer is used to hearing.

❏ Relocation; jobs you have experience with do not exist in new area.

❏ Completed education or training; now qualified for position.

❏ Lack of growth, opportunity, promotion, recognition.

❏ New area of emerging growth with greater possibilities for career.

❏ Part of long-range plan.

❏ Long-time interest, dream, or ambition.

❏ Time was right due to other changes in personal/professional life. (Such as industry downturn, layoffs, store closings or other factors totally out of your control.)

Negative Reasons for Change
Or what you should not say in the interview.

❏ Best friend got job here so now I am looking too.

❏ Neat office, nice perks, great salary.

❏ Saw the ad.

❏ I need a new life.

❏ That &@$*&$^*@ company—I hated it there.

❏ That &*@$(^$ manager—I had to get out.

❏ Not learning; not challenging; not interesting. I was bored.

❏ Burnt-out.

❏ My horoscope advised a change.

❏ ? (Not able to articulate any reasons.)

Job-Hoppers

Who is a job-hopper? People who work in industries or professions where it is the norm to move around and have many different employers over a period of time. Think short-term construction, theater arts, video editing, graphic arts, and computer programming, for example. Interviewers would not look twice at a job candidate with a streak of jobs in a variety of organizations in such professions; it would not seem unusual to have the average job tenure be less than 1 year for each employer. It is a case of finishing a project or assignment and moving on. In a high-tech job, it is not unusual to see a lot of turnover created by the strong demand.

For other job seekers who are job hoppers, it might have been a series of bad luck: Employer 1 went out of business; Employer 2 could not generate enough business to cover costs and laid off workers; Employer 3 was simply a rotten place to work; you moved to Employer 4 in desperation and are extremely dissatisfied with the lack of opportunities for advancement. Again, when reviewing your decisions, you should be able to explain them to the satisfaction of an interviewer.

Situation: I was terminated after a 90-day probationary period. How do I explain? I quit my last job because I needed more money. This makes three jobs in 4 years. How do I explain this?

If you were terminated after 30, 60, or 90 days by your last employer, you need to be prepared to respond to the question asked. However, don't share more information then you need to. For any employment of short-term duration, consider—as we discussed above—omitting any mention on the résumé (as we said, though you may have to include it on the employment application). If you are going to include it, then try to give it a positive spin and always avoid any negative feelings toward the employer or any of its individuals.

It just didn't work out. The job portrayed during recruitment was different from the one I was expected to perform. In all fairness to them it wasn't their fault. The market changed abruptly.

I quit my last job because I needed more money. It was a great job but I was driving 78 miles each way every day and when my car broke down, I realized I was unable to afford the _____ daily cost it was going to be to get to work.

This makes three jobs in four years. I know it seems like a lot of job-hopping but one employer relocated to Mexico. The second was sold and my position was determined to be redundant and so now I am in my third job.

Continuity of Experience

If your work history is varied and seemingly disconnected, look for continuity in your responsibilities and duties. What skills did you use in your previous jobs? What did you learn from the variety of employers? What other benefits have you reaped from these experiences: did you deal with different industries, types of people, or procedures? Job-hopping can be sold as another type of on-the-job training, packing a lot of experience into a short time frame if you can identify the common denominators and the transferable skills. Review your reasons for changing jobs: why did you accept and then why did you leave each position? Did you plan it that way or did it just happen?

For example, a bank lending officer takes maternity leave and then decides not to return to full-time employment when the leave ends. A neighbor runs a business out of his home and needs bookkeeping services on a part-time basis. She begins to work for him. News of her offering this service gets around, and several other people approach her to do financial work for them. She decides to open her own business, offering financial services out of her home. Soon her spouse is assigned to another state, and the family moves. She takes a job as a treasurer for the nursery school her child attends. When her child moves on to kindergarten, she begins to look for full-time employment.

Here is a summary of her work history:

Bank lending officer	5 years
Bookkeeper for neighbor	8 months
Own business	14 months
Unemployed	2 months
Nursery school	9 months

She has had continuity in financial duties and has learned to file her own payroll taxes as well as to use several financial and banking software packages. In 5 years she has had four different employment situations— each with a logical explanation.

Career Goals

The best way to advance your career is by taking a proactive approach:

❏ Seek opportunities that advance your career goals.
❏ Know your core values and beliefs.
❏ Understand your needs.
❏ Learn the needs of your employer.

Look over all the jobs that you have held and the reasons you took and left each position. Now, where are you heading? Is the next job—the one you are interviewing for currently—a step in the right direction or a detour? Is it your goal or a means to an end?

Continuity of Experience

List your top five selling points—the skills that qualify you for the job opening—and then list the different jobs that utilized those skills. Provide one example of how you used each skill.

Skill: _____

   Job(s): _____

          _____

   Example: _____

Skill: _____

   Job(s): _____

          _____

   Example: _____

Skill: _____

   Job(s): _____

          _____

   Example: _____

Skill: _____

   Job(s): _____

          _____

   Example: _____

Skill: _____

   Job(s): _____

          _____

   Example: _____

Situation: Your long-term goal is to be a graphic artist, and you have been taking classes for the last year on weekends and during the evening. You know you are not ready to interview for this type of position yet, nor can you afford to take an internship or a low-paying trainee job right now. In a year or two, this is a move you will likely make. Meanwhile, you are working as a buyer for a department store, and there is an opportunity for a promotion and an increase in salary but you must interview for the position. How do you answer questions about your classes and career goals?

Do you plan to give your employer 100 percent of your effort on the job? No one asks you to promise to work for life! Most employment is voluntary. You can be fired at any time for a good reason, a bad reason, or no reason (but not an illegal reason). Provided your classes do not interfere with your day job, it need not be revealed in an interview. You can control disclosure; your after-hour pursuits are personal. And, who knows? You may change your mind in a year or so. What you decide now is not written in stone. So, if you are asked about your career goals, you can honestly respond in the following way:

> *This is a great opportunity for me to learn more about the retail market and work with talented managers. I hope to be able to take advantage of it. This will give me a chance to expand on the knowledge that I have acquired.*

Get a Plan for Your Career

❏ What is your most immediate professional problem?

❏ What are your immediate objectives? Long-term plans?

❏ What are all the possible solutions or alternatives?

❏ What would be the probable consequences or logical conclusions to these alternatives?

❏ What would be the trade-offs or costs of these alternatives?

❏ What is your approach to risk-taking?

❏ How do you feel about uncertainty?

❏ What actions can you take today? What must you do to prepare to take action now?

Questions

12.1 What are your special abilities?

This is one more question that your skills inventory should make you a pro at answering. Pick two or three work-related abilities that you are particularly proud of and traits that your interviewer will appreciate hearing about.

I have the uncanny ability of getting to the issues and then getting everyone to agree with what is needed to resolve them.

I am able to write down a complicated problem, break it down into manageable components, and state it on one page.

I have the old-fashioned belief that once you promise something, you deliver.

12.2 Of all the places you have worked as a _____, which one gave you the most opportunities to grow?

With your personal inventory as part of your preparation, this is a good question for you to answer. Tell your story briefly, and try to relate it to the organization where you are interviewing.

That has to be the time I spent at XYZ Corporation. I was fortunate to work for a great person who served as a mentor. Additionally, the company was really growing, so there were opportunities all over and we really seized them. In fact it was that growth that makes me particularly ready for the situation you have described here.

12.3 At which of these employers do you feel you made the greatest contribution?

A "gimme," but be careful because you need to show what will appear to be a significant contribution to the interviewer.

I made the greatest contribution at LMN, because it was there that I designed a pension plan that is still in effect today.

12.4 Why are you not seeking to be rehired by one of your former employers?

As a matter of fact, I am talking to one of my former employers who is very interested in having me return.

Or

I feel I have progressed each time I left one job and organization for another. If I return to any of the organizations where I worked before, rightly or wrongly, I feel that I would be taking a step backward. If any of them had a position that represented a real challenge for me, I would certainly pursue the opportunity.

12.5 You have a degree. Don't you think this position is a bit below your capabilities?

My degree is a confirmation of the fact that I completed the requirements for school. The skills required to do that are different from those you described for the position here. I do feel, however, that the intellectual capacity evidenced by my degree is an indication of what I bring to the job.

12.6 What specific skills that you acquired or used in your last job relate specifically to this one?

For starters, the analytical skills I developed on my past job will help me to be effective here because I take a problem-solving approach to my work. Second, we had a sense of urgency in all that we did there. Third, we had a customer focus—one more detail that I feel will be very relevant here. Did I leave anything out?

12.7 How would you feel about reporting to someone who would have been your subordinate in your last position?

This position represents a whole other dimension. It is one in which the person who would have been a subordinate in different circumstances would actually be my superior here. It makes sense because in this environment I need to seek out the person who is more familiar with the nature of the work.

12.8 What do I tell my people who will feel that you are a threat to their job security if you work here?

You need to tell them that it is not the case. If they feel that way, they need to meet with you to discuss their reasons.

12.9 You seem to be used to bigger issues than you will face here. How can I trust that you will not leave as soon as a more challenging job comes along?

Bigger does not always mean better. I am very impressed with the environment and the team here, as well as the opportunity—and the challenge—of the job itself. If this were not true, I would not be talking to you seriously about this job. You can see from my work history that I am not a job hopper. If you offer me the opportunity to work for you in the position that we have been talking about, I see no reason to become one now.

13

Over 50?

"I Am Not *that* Old"

When considering age as an aspect of your job search, you need to consider it from two perspectives:

Chronological: How old are you physically and how old do you look physically? In U.S. culture today, fitness and youth are major issues regardless of your birth date. Appearance enhances image, and image enhances confidence.

Professional age: Where are you in your profession? Are you in the early stages? Are you at the midlevel—some seasoning but still growing? Are you at an advanced level—seasoned, at the top of your game, on top of everything that is happening, and staying current. Are you at the senior levels of the organization, considered a major contributor and admired by peers and colleagues—inside and outside your organization? Or are you burned out? Or are you obsolete professionally? Has your career stopped advancing and your skills are those of yesterday or last year?

Recently, a national TV cable network was looking for a video broadcast designer. The network decided to conduct a dual search; it was looking for seasoned professionals who could "hit the ground running," and it was also willing to consider recent college graduates who "had a good creative eye." For anyone to qualify, experience with After Effects software was required. If you didn't have it, your profession had passed you by regardless of chronological age and professional experience.

From the Perspective of the Interviewer

Consider the issue of age from the interviewer's perspective. A key question is how important is the candidate's age to the interviewer? Are you and the interviewer similar in age? Do you appear old enough to be his or her mother or father? Age is a complicated issue. Younger generations have more differences among one another than they do with the over-50 generation.

Stereotypes

Stereotyping based on age is not uncommon. Even though age discrimination is legally protected, it is hard for employers not to exhibit some bias. If you are over 50, be conscious of it and do what you can to deal with any job situation.

Human resources departments are places you will probably have to deal with it. In that area, there are a lot of younger people early in their careers. If you need to deal with them, do so from the perspective of one who knows less about their organization than they do. Allow them to do their jobs, and remain flexible.

Employment agencies and executive recruiters are other opportunities to tread lightly. There are two potential problems here. First, they assume they need youth because that is going to make them look good in the eyes of the client. Second, they don't know any better because frequently they are young themselves.

Labor Pool

The labor market (in some areas) favors age and experience. When the job market is tight, there are more opportunities for older workers. In fact, enlightened employers do realize that there are benefits to gain from older workers—things like work ethic, loyalty, experience, and know-how. This awareness, however, is not universal. Some employers may try to exploit older workers. For example, a commercial bank in New York City attempted to hire a very senior credit officer by asking him to include his retirement pay (he was eligible for his pension) as part of his compensation from them. What the bank was trying to do in effect was get him at a discount by paying him less than the market rate, hoping he would see that his pension was part of his pay regardless of where it was coming from. Needless to say, it didn't work, and he ended up receiving a premium above his previous pay rate.

Why should any employer pay a premium for experience? Or is it that older workers are overpaid? The real answer is, *"It depends."* Are you someone who performed the same activities 20,000 times as you worked for the same employer 20 years in a row? Or did you learn something new each year? Frequently in this job market, positions that have had little if any turnover will probably be paid below the market rate. On the other hand, if you worked for a sophisticated employer who did not want his or her employees to quit, it is quite possible that you are being paid above the market rate because you got a merit increase every year. Now the job is priced above the market rate, so it would be cheaper to replace you with someone greener—and less expensive.

The key question is, what is the quality of your experience? You need to take a detailed and realistic look at yourself to come up with an answer. Evaluate yourself:

❑ What language do you speak? Is it the language of contemporaries in your field? Do the latest jargon and acronyms mean anything to you?

❑ Are you current? Even if you have not worked for a cutting-edge employer, have you kept up on your own? Are you informed about the latest and the greatest ideas and sources in your profession?

❑ What is your work history like? Have you worked for just one employer for the past 10 (or more!) years? If you have, you probably have enormous knowledge but is it only based on one organization? After high school, a woman joined a major bank as a clerk. She was extremely successful and received many promotions; eventually she established a career as a human resources professional. She kept moving up the organization ladder in the HR track. The bank went through two mergers. After the second merger, her $80,000 a year job was eliminated, and she was given a generous severance package. However, she wanted to continue her career. It wasn't long before she realized that other organizations weren't looking for HR professionals who had come up through the ranks at one major financial institution but who didn't have a college degree and who had very little other experience.

How to Price Yourself.

When we speak of price, we are really speaking of the annual salary you want or need. Price is a difficult but necessary item to quantify. It is complex because whatever price you quote must be stated with confidence—no waffling, no hedging (*"I am flexible"* or *"It's negotiable"*). State your price and then be quiet. Coming up with the right number is the problem.

Value-Added—Trade-offs

You need to consider yourself in terms of what value you bring to the organization. Branding is the common name for it these days. A level of confidence needs to emanate from you that says, *"I am good at what I do and I really can help this organization by _____."* To get to this point, you need to consider what there is about you that will be of value to the organization.

In human resources, for instance, if an organization needs to hire a lot of people, demonstrate your skill in finding sources for appropriate people. In sales, what have you done to demonstrate you skill in selling? You need to show that you are worth your price tag and that hiring you will result in positives (that is, value-added) for the employer.

What Is the Right Amount for You?

Say you were making $75,000 and the organization you were in gave you a considerable increase and bonus combination so the new total is now close to $100,000. Then you were let go. You talk to a recruiter who presents a job to you that is paying no more than $80,000. Should you consider it? Before answering no because you don't want to take a cut in pay, you need to determine what the value of the pay level is in this organization versus the value in the one you just left. Among the items that will add to or detract from your pay level are the following:

❑ What is your compensation on an hourly basis? To calculate this, compute your hourly rate based on the total number of hours you put in per week plus the time it takes you to get to and from work. Use the following formula:

> Total hours = Total average number of hours spent weekly at work + the time it takes you to get to and from work (weekly) + any other time you are expected to be available.

> Then, to calculate your hourly wage, divide your annual compensation by the total number of hours you work all year based on the formula above, or

$$\frac{\text{Total annual compensation}}{(\text{Tot. weekly hours spent working} + \text{Tot. weekly travel time} + \text{Tot. weekly other work trip time}) \times 52 \text{ Weeks}} = \text{Hourly Wage}$$

❑ Factor in the incidental costs. A long commute is not cheap, either in the use of your time or in the actual expenses of a train ticket, taxis, or gasoline. Comparing a 2-hour commute by a combination of rail and bus with a 15-minute drive entails different expenses which must be considered. If it costs you $18,000 a year in commutation to earn the

$100,000 salary, then the $80,000 offered in the above example is not that far out of line. It can also work in the reverse, costing you $18,000 for the $80,000 job. Other incidentals can include the need to buy a cell phone for your commute, shopping for a new wardrobe, and the affect on your lifestyle.

How to Successfully Compete with Younger, Cheaper Candidates

Identify Selling Points

What do you have that makes you unique to your potential employer? This includes your experience and proven abilities backed up with proven results. Review Chapter 6 for self-assessment.

Differentiate Yourself

Set yourself apart from your potential competition. Who is your most likely competition? What will be the profile of the other candidates that respond to the opening? If there is an ad or better yet a posting on the Internet, it will be filled with details that frequently encourage a more youthful candidate. If you read "5 years experience," consider this a hint.

Determine whether the level of responsibility is appropriate for you at the current point in your career. Consider the specific words that describe the nature and scope of the job responsibilities. Also, look at the title of the person the position reports to if it is available. When you are deciding to respond, don't give up (unless the scope and level as described seems very low), but don't boast about your 25-year career either. Rather identify key accomplishments and perhaps consider a functional résumé that emphasizes your accomplishments over years. If the organization needs someone to build a sales team and you have done that, then make the point and demonstrate what that sales team accomplished. Great sales people are very successful in making sales, but great sales people are not always skilled at putting a team together.

Recognize disadvantages in what you have to offer. A big disadvantage is age *if* the organization seems predisposed to youth. Don't deny it, but work to dispel the bias. Why is youth regarded as an advantage? Is it knowing the latest technology? Show that you have kept up by using the latest terms and expressions. Furthermore, young people are perceived as having a lot of energy. Frequently, employers perceive people early in their careers as "hungry" (that is, willing to do anything because they really want to succeed) and unencumbered (people just out of college can start right away, have very little to move, and have no outside conflicts) so they will be able to work a hundred hours a week. How do you prove you are loaded with energy? Stay (or get) fit. Avoid alcohol at any employer-sponsored meal. Don't take a smoking break unless you are applying for a job at Phillip Morris. Don't talk about your vacation home (or time share). Don't mention that your real love is golf (or sailing). If you feel it appropriate, share the fact that spending more than three days on a beach is something you are totally unable to comprehend.

You should also take into account the culture of the organization with respect to the ages of its employees. You may not want to work in the equivalent of a retirement village, but would you want to work with a majority of Generation Y employees? What biases are you harboring? What do you know, from reading and your own experience, of people of different age groups? How are they alike and how are they different? The current generation may have more in common with the baby boomer generation than the one in-between, Generation X. An additional consideration is diversity; if you have been working for years with people from the neighborhood and now you are faced with a virtual United Nations, how will you cope? (For further discussion of age issues, read *Generations at Work,* Zemke, Raines, and Filipczak. AMACOM New York 2000.)

Facing the Questions Successfully

The key to success on an interview is to be fresh, vibrant, and prepared. One advantage you have over any younger competition is right there at the interview. You know that if anything can go wrong, it will. So you plan accordingly. The building the interview is in has three different lobbies. You need to go to the reception area off the lobby to check in before you can go up to your meeting, and it seems that everyone on earth is trying to get into this building at the same time, you can handle it because you made a test visit there last week. And

Because you are sharp and confident.

Because you really want to work for this organization and you are not going to let your guard down while you make sure that the interviewer knows that you really want to work here.

Because you are going to write up your notes of the meeting as soon as you can and before you forget what just occurred.

Because you are going to write a thank-you note as soon as you get out.

Because of all these reasons, you are going to succeed.

Questions

13.1   What if you find out that your boss is biased? He or she prefers one of your colleagues, even though you've performed better.

Be ready for this one. It won't get asked too often—only when it is relevant to the organization where you are interviewing. It has just experienced this situation and may even be getting sued.

I would not come to such a serious conclusion very quickly. It is difficult to imagine because it has never happened to me. In the unlikely event that I did come to this conclusion, I would request a meeting with my supervisor and let him or her know that I feel I have been performing at a better level than my colleague. How does he or she feel? I would then try to determine my supervisor's reasons for choosing another over me. If I continued to feel that his or her decision was unjustified, I would let him or her know and see what he or she says in response to my inquiry. I would then ask about what, in his or her opinion, are areas where I could use further development.

13.2   After 6 months on this job, what will be the most annoying thing about you?

This very imaginative question may cause problems if you fail to respond quickly and confidently. It is a complex variation of the question, "What is your weakness?" As with the question answered in our earlier *Best Answers* book, you need to identify a trait that while laudatory to some may be annoying to others.

I always wear the latest clothes.

Or

I always work on the commuter train instead of engaging in conversation with other commuters.

13.3   Could we see some ID (passport, driver's license, Social Security card)?

This is a touchy question because the interviewer may be using it as a ploy to find out how old you really are. Legally, you do not have to show identification until it is time to fill out an I-9 (after you have commenced work for an employer) or you are applying for a job that requires some form of government clearance. The real question is whether you want to be subjected to the questions arising from either your refusal to provide ID or, in doing so, reveal your age.

I am sorry but I got a lift here today, and I do not have my license with me.

13.4 *Why are you coming out of retirement? (If this fact has been previously revealed to explain a gap in employment.)*

Well, after I retired, I relaxed. I traveled. I read. And I got bored. I realized that I loved selling medical supplies. I was great at it. Clients seemed to feel I had an "old-time credibility" and I certainly had a reputation for delivering the goods as promised. I can still do the reading, and travel has always been a part of the job. So I want to use my skills and at the same time enjoy meeting new people in a new organization. Who knows, some of my old customers might follow me here!

13.5 *Do coworkers listen to your ideas?*

There may be a hint of bias here from the interviewer, with the possible insinuation that you may not have many ideas—let alone ideas worth listening to. Despite this, you are going to respond to this question energetically and with confidence and excitement in your voice.

Absolutely. They seem to value the knowledge I have obtained from the experience I have. I do not believe in reinventing the wheel, and I constantly like to make suggestions to encourage them to do the same. Sometimes, it surprises me how the most simple ideas are never considered. For instance, I was invited to join a creative bunch of employees on the roof of our building to consider a problem. The issue was that they wanted to fly an American flag and a corporate flag but there was only one flagpole and no one could think of a solution. I was going to make a suggestion but hesitated because I thought surely it had already been considered. "What about a second flagpole"? I suggested. Everyone thought it was a great idea and wondered why they hadn't thought of it sooner.

13.6 *Do you ever doubt your abilities? Your decisions?*

I feel that there is a big difference between doubting abilities and doubting decisions. If every decision you make is correct, chances are you are not making enough decisions.

On the other hand, the interviewer needs assurance that you never doubt your abilities.

One of the keys to my effectiveness in the workplace and my success to date is my ability to work with others to always find a solution. I tend to ponder an issue or problem and then go to solid sources to seek advice. Based on research, I come to a solid conclusion. The decisions do not always pan out (sometimes, for instance, the technology changes or new competition arrives) but the process to get to those decisions is rock solid.

13.7 Tell me about a time when you had to make a fast decision.

This is a great follow-up question.

Even though we have regularly scheduled maintenance on our equipment, one day the copy machine quit working. A repair order was put in, and the repair worker would be on site in a few hours. However, a major marketing mailing was being prepared and had to go out that afternoon. I packed up what was already copied and the masters, envelopes, and postage. A crew came with me to the local Kinko's. I had called ahead, and the Kinko's staff was ready for us. With their assistance (and my credit card), we got the mailing out and were back in the office to greet the repair person. I took this action even though I had not received prior approval to incur the expense. Time was of the essence, and I acted accordingly.

13.8 Tell me about a time when you made a decision that turned out to be wrong.

That is easy. Buying the copy machine in the first place! I had done the research and compared contracts and prices, thinking that this was the best deal. We even had a test machine for 2 weeks. As soon as the trial period was over, the problems began. After many months of struggling to get the machine to work properly, since I had recommended the purchase, I contacted the president of the manufacturer and lodged a complaint. I made more telephone calls to follow up. Shortly thereafter (I think just to end my telephoning them), they replaced the machine with a different model that worked, but productivity on our end had suffered for several months.

13.9 What do you think is the hardest part of working with people who are much younger than you?

Be careful. Turn this into a positive if you can.

I need to be realistic about their lifestyle interests. Frequently, but not always, there is also a work ethic that is more varied than what I am used to. The fact is that they are sometimes distracted by personal situations. My biggest challenge is getting them to concentrate on their work and realize how important they are to the enterprise.

13.10 What do you think is the hardest part of working for people younger than you? What is the biggest challenge in dealing with younger people in the workplace (employees, customers, suppliers)?

It is no big deal, but one issue comes to mind. They frequently are vague about what they want accomplished. They also send conflicting messages. By seeking clarification from the start, everyone knows what is expected.

13.11   *You see someone younger than you performing a task that you know you could do better. What is your reaction?*

My first thought is to see if that person is maximizing his or her time. I would ask if he or she would like some help. If the answer is no, I then look for an opportunity to make a suggestion and see how it goes over. The best training is that which is not perceived to be training at all. I get personal satisfaction from providing help if it is wanted and then seeing the person I've trained accomplish tasks as well if not better than I could.

13.12   *Most of our staff is older/younger than you. How will you fit in?*

No problem. Age is a part of the healthy diversification of the workplace. We will all learn from one another. In fact some of the younger workers frequently are more at odds with each other than with older ones.

13.13   *Do you know how to use a _____ (machine/software/technical device)?*

Yes, I have had some experience with it. What will I need to accomplish with it?

If necessary add *"a little coaching would get me up to speed quickly."*

Or

No, I don't. But I would like to see what you need me to do with it so that I could let you know how quickly I could be up to speed and what it would take to get me there.

If you don't have a clue, be honest and say so. *No, I don't. What portion of the job is dependent on that skill?*

13.14   *When did you last get a promotion/increase?*

One reason for asking this question is to determine whether you are about to get an increase. If you are, the organization would need to know so that a reasonable offer could be made. One human resources professional swears that everyone he ever tries to hire is always just about to get an increase, a promotion, or both. On the other hand, watch out that it hasn't been too long (more than 12 months for an increase).

13.15   *What was your last evaluation like?*

Be careful here. If you are in one of these organizations that insists that evaluations be consistent with the "normal curve" of distribution, you more likely than not will fall into the average or middle category. Be sure to provide a brief clarification up front. If you have received any accolades, be sure to include those comments. Be brief, though. The less said, the better. If you haven't had an evaluation in quite a while, say so. Many organizations are not consistent when their employees are evaluated, so many managers avoid them if at all possible. Watch out though because it is a small world, and your interviewer may have a different understanding of your organization's evaluation policy.

13.16 Do you own a computer (PC/Mac)?

This is an "are you with it?" question. If you answer affirmatively, be prepared to speak knowledgeably when you describe what you do with it. In any event, do not try to fake it. You run the very real risk of fumbling badly if you do.

As long as I had access to one when I needed it, I did not feel the need to purchase one. However, I would like to do more personal business with a computer such as online banking and research. So I plan to purchase an iMac in the next few weeks.

13.17 What programs do you use the most? Why?

Any business-related software—a combined E-mail, word processing, general ledger, presentation, and database software package is ideal (for example, Microsoft Office). If you don't need any of them at work, you should take it upon yourself to learn each of these to see what a personal computer can do for you. Then if you would like to show that you are really a techie, you could also mention other software you use including electronic banking and bill paying. You should also include your proficiency on the Internet. It is hard to imagine a professional person anywhere who is PC ignorant. If this is you, start to learn right away and use practical applications to see how effective the PC will make you right from the start.

13.18 Do you prefer working in an office alone, sharing an office, or working in a common area?

The best approach is to demonstrate your willingness to be flexible.

I can work effectively in any surroundings. All three have their advantages. In the course of my career, I have had the benefit of experiencing each.

If your job requires you to get around, you should add "*I really like to get out and be with my clients/direct reports/colleagues as much as possible, so I try not to stay behind the desk very long.*"

13.19 *Do you use the Internet? For what purpose(s)?*

If you say yes, be prepared for follow-up questions. (If you say no, then "Why not?" will crop up.) Do you use it at home? Work? Both? How many hours daily for each? What do you use it for?

If you use it for personal information (travel, restaurants, esoteric hobbies, genealogy) that is okay, but be sure to include some business-related reasons as well. If you are responsible for purchasing in your organization and you tried to do it on the Web, say so and share your experience— whether humbling or effective. You can also expand your answer with new skills you recently learned while conducting your job search.

> *I recently discovered how easy it is to store and use my work files online. This service www._____.com provides free storage as well as a calendar, reminder services, and fax messaging. It has become my new home page.*

If you have no experience online, you will probably be expected to elaborate.

> *I am eagerly waiting to take a class at _____ on using the Internet. My former employer was not into technology, but I feel that it cannot be ignored. Once I am proficient, I will get a modem for my home PC.*

And you can follow-up with, *"How does this organization use the Internet?" "Are all employees able to access the company Intranet?"*

13.20 *Have you been to our Website? Please give me your comments—what did you like and dislike?*

This is one more question that you can expect to be asked in this line of questioning. Before you go to the interview, there is no excuse for you not to spend some time with the company's Website just as you should, we suppose, eat its candy bar before going on an interview with a candy maker. In response to, "What did you think?" most people will say that it was a very nice Website. The astute interviewer may not ask what you disliked but, "What could we do better?" instead. If your job is going to be involved in new media, then that is all the more reason to be knowledgeable and do your research before going to the interview.

13.21 *What can you do for us that someone else can't?*

The interviewer is giving you a great opportunity to sell yourself.

> *What I do is not rocket science nor is accounting or swimming. Yet the way to become proficient at any of these activities is by doing them. I have become*

an expert in _____ because of the unique set of experiences that I bring to the table and a track record of accomplishment that says I could hit the ground running and quickly achieve results for you.

13.22   *What can you teach your coworkers?*

Leading by example is something I can do. With the experience I have, I can pretty much face any situation and know how to deal with it. My coworkers will quickly appreciate my instincts and experience since these are things they cannot learn in school. With me as a role model, they will quickly see the importance of growing in responsibility and profit from every experience they face. The other thing I will provide is a real passion for the company and my work. The more I am in this field, the more lucky I feel I am to have found this profession. This feeling will become infectious and will wear on each member of my unit—in a positive, energizing way—as well.

14

You Have the Floor

Interviews are a two-way street. You know you will probably be asked, *"Do you have any questions?"* Raising questions for the sake of raising questions is not the name of the game. Ideally, the interview should have progressed into a business discussion with give-and-take on both sides of the desk. As topics are raised, questions do come to mind and additional information is sought. A good interviewer will do this—follow up on your comments and seek further details. A good interviewee should do the same.

The Best Questions Are Those that Did Not Have to Be Asked

When there is reciprocity and a flow to the conversation, both parties informally take turns controlling the interview. After rapport is established, either party should feel comfortable redirecting the flow of conversation and initiating topics. Remember that the interviewer's agenda must be met before you can introduce your agenda.

Being properly prepared for an interview means you have done your homework. You have information about the job and the organization, and you are able to put yourself into the mind of the interviewer. When you have insight into what the organization needs to fill the job opening, you can relate your qualifications even if you are not asked to do so directly. You have prepared your agenda. Consider your main selling points. What if the interviewer neglects to ask "the question" that allows you to go into further details about them? Perhaps the interviewer is not aware of the relevance of these skills for the job; he or she may be relying on an inadequate or nonexistent job description. If you are not asked something—and it is essential to your candidacy—bring it up yourself either by asking a question that relates to it or pointing out a reference to it on your résumé. For example, *"Would I be required to write periodic reports? That is what I thought. At _____ Company the reports I created were a great way to review the performance of the unit as well as to consider improvements. One report I wrote regarding _____ allowed the company to initiate a new record keeping system that saved both time and money."*

When to Ask Questions

You will have to get a feel for your interviewer and the flow of conversation in order to determine when to ask your questions. An interviewer who favors a structured interview may not wish the interview's rhythm interrupted, particularly if he or she has a list of basic questions to get through. However, if the interviewer asks a question that you do not understand or raises an issue that requires more elaboration, raise your question(s) while you are on the topic.

> *Since you mentioned the importance of timely reporting, I would like to mention that it was necessary for me to collect information on a regular basis from several divisions at _____ to prepare the weekly sales quota reports. I made this a much quicker and easier process by accessing databases directly through the Intranet, not having to wait for department heads to send the information to me. What is the process used here?*

Another opportunity to raise questions is when it is apparent that the interviewer is changing topics. *"Before we go on to my technical background, I would like to point out that I had the wonderful opportunity to attend a seminar 2 days ago on the subject of _____, which fits right in with your organization's current product line."* Now, you have dangled an enticing subject in front of the interviewer: Will he or she pick up on it? The natural follow up to your statement would be, *"Really? What was covered in the seminar?"*

One reason for your asking questions is to see how intuitive and clued in the interviewer is. You deserve the same right to rate the interviewer (and by default the organization) as the interviewer has to rate you. The other reason to ask questions is that you need the information to either form further responses or to provide sufficient information for you to decide, if an offer were made, whether you would accept it.

Feedback Questions

A great technique for taking the pulse of the interview as you go is to check yourself out along the way and draw out the interviewer.

> *. . . And that is how I solved that technical problem. Did I answer your question, or do you wish further details?*

Another way to get feedback is to repeat or rephrase the question you are asked.

> *Let me see if I understand the situation. What would I do if my supervisor gave most of the staff time off for a long weekend and there was a deadline to meet?*

This technique will allow you a moment or two to formulate an answer as well as to be certain that you are answering the right question.

When You Are Asking the Questions . . .

❑ Connect the dots ahead of time before you open a topic. If you bring up the subject, can it lead to your being asked questions that you would rather not get into?

❑ Employ tact to get employed. If there have been unfavorable news stories (*"What is up with the illegal dumping anyway?"*), do not dwell on the issue unless it is one that directly involves your prospective job. (*"As the safety officer, what would be my responsibility toward trash removal?"*)

❑ Enjoy the quiet moments. It you open up with idle chatter because you cannot deal with silence, you may say more than you intend.

❑ Stay under the protection of illegal subjects; if you feel that your religious background could be a negative issue, do not bring up the subject of where you attend services and whom you have met there. If your contact was through a political group, there is no need to reveal any additional information other than you know each other socially.

❑ Do not ask questions that you should have known or found out before you decided to go on the interview. This will reveal your lack of research and interest.

How to Ask Questions

One word to avoid is *"Why."* It can often seem confrontational and may trigger a negative response. Rather than saying, *"Why did you drop the children's clothing line?"* try, *"I am interested in the organization's recent decision to drop the children's clothing line. Could we discuss that for a moment?"* This does not mean that you will not be asked a lot of "why" questions—the interviewer is interested in your decisions and actions and wants to understand how your mind works. This is the role that interviewers have cast themselves into—one that may seem that they are judging and second-guessing your motivation and actions.

If you have made a list of questions or key points to cover in advance, ask if you may refer to your notes.

> *When I was visiting your Website, I had a few questions that I wrote down. Do you mind if I refer to my notes?*
>
> *There was so much information available through magazine articles and newspapers that I took notes. I was particularly interested in the newsletter the Website offered.*

Questions You Must Ask (or Know the Answers to Already)

You need to have enough information about the organization and the job opening so that you can make a decision if the job were to be offered to you. That would include the basics:

❏ Management, management style, organizational profile

❏ Operations, finances, current developments, plans

❏ Job description, incumbent, career path, review schedule

❏ How long the job has been open, hiring procedures, decision time frame

On the first interview, do not bring up the subject of compensation, benefits, vacation, health plans, or other similar issues. When the interviewer goes into a "sell" mode, these ancillary issues may be introduced as reasons why you should want the job. Similarly, until the organization is ready to make an offer, the subject of your salary history and requirements should be forestalled. (For information on subsequent interviews, see Chapter 16, Offers and Negotiations.)

Answers and Information You Need	
List, by category, the information you need or questions that you must ask in the interview.	
Categories	**Questions and Information Needed**
Position	
Organization	
Management	
Operations/goals	
Other	

Do not seem apologetic about asking questions. You deserve the right to know what you may be getting into. In fact, the interviewer should have covered the basics when he or she entered the selling mode—selling both the job and the organization to you. Ideally, you should only be filling in some gaps in information between your research and what was revealed in the interview itself.

Upping the Stakes

If you are invited back for additional interviews, it is expected that

❑ You have done some additional research into the organization.

❑ You have retained and reviewed the information covered in prior interviews.

❑ You are prepared to go over material covered earlier for different people with different points of view.

❑ You are prepared to provide further details and insights into your skills and experience, particularly in relationship to this organization and job opening.

❑ You will have more questions for the interviewer(s).

You may be meeting with senior management, department or division heads, potential coworkers, or team members; some organizations even get their employees involved in the interviewing process, seeking hiring input from them about future coworkers. These additional interviews may be completely different in tone and scope from the prior interview(s), so do not be lulled into a false sense of security. Research, rehearse, and relax for each one! There should be a sense of coming together and mutuality of purpose with these subsequent interviews, and the subject of compensation may certainly be initiated at any time.

Compensation Questions

On the first interview. Since there are no hard-and-fast rules governing interviews, some interviewers may press for information about your current salary level or what your price tag will be even though they know you probably will not want to reveal it and they are nowhere near making a job offer. If this happens, it is most likely to exclude from or include you for further consideration. The trick is to keep your candidacy alive (if you like what you have heard so far). If you are not totally impressed but sheer dollars would make you look twice, roll the dice and state what you are looking for.

Here is a question from the employer. "We are only paying $____, and that is lower than your current base salary. Would you take a cut in pay to take this job?" The earlier in the interview process it is, the weaker your position. The question may be used to screen out candidates, and salary is a major consideration. There are several alternative ways to respond. The first and weakest is, *"Yes, I would because I want so much to work for this organization."* A second alternative may end the conversation and the opportunity: *"I would not be willing to do that."* A third alternative would be to say:

> *Even though my base is higher with my current employer, I would like to evaluate the entire compensation package, including benefits, if and when you make an offer. Quite frankly, my understanding is that your benefits and some other aspects of the compensation package (opportunity for overtime/bonus, 401(K) match, a pension, annual reviews) may make the total package a competitive one, even if the base salary is lower than what I currently make.*

Before saying any of these things, you need to be sure you have an accurate understanding of the compensation and benefits package that the organization you are meeting with currently offers. One more alternative is to say, *"In the short term, I am willing to take a pay cut if I must because the long-term career prospects look so good here and I so want to work for this organization."* If you want, you may also decide to add, *"I really believe in it and what it stands for."*

Regardless of when this issue is raised, always remember that you are not making a commitment to join them when they pop this question, so don't feel that the matter is closed and that you have agreed to join them at that base salary. If this discussion happens before an offer is actually made, a lot could happen, and the organization could up the ante when an offer is really made. If you show flexibility here, you continue as a prospect. If the organization shows that it doesn't know how to negotiate, perhaps it is just as well if it drops you from consideration.

"What salary are you now earning? What was your last salary level? What salary are you looking for? How much would it take to get you to change jobs?"

> *I am earning mid-six figures, exclusive of bonuses and other compensation elements and would consider a lateral move if there were a signing bonus or an early review date offered.*

That is direct and the ball is now in their court. Or you just might consider asking, *"What is your salary level for similar positions?"* You can try to get a clue of what the pay scale is. You could also consider:

> In recent advertisements for similar positions at other organizations, I have seen low six-figure salaries being offered. That seems about right, but it does not take into consideration the entire compensation package.

You have hedged your bet and left room for negotiation, yet you have not revealed what you are currently earning.

In a subsequent interview. If asked about your salary requirements in a subsequent interview, you might say, *Oh! Are you offering me the job?* Now that brings the conversation to the point but is a win-lose ploy. If the interviewer says, *"No, not at this point,"* you can always proceed with one of the answers offered above.

Questions for You to Ask

How long have you worked here?

Can you describe your organizational culture?

Do you have a lot of turnover? Why/why not? What has the turnover been for this position/this department?

The question about turnover is an important one to ask any employer you are considering. When you ask, you need to know how to evaluate the answer. Watch out for the organization that has managers and human resource representatives who unashamedly will say, *"I don't know."* If responsible people are not knowledgeable about this very important barometer, it is either because they don't want to know because they have a revolving-door problem or, worse, don't know that they should want to know.

If turnover is too low, it may mean that the organization for whatever reason is retaining "deadwood"—not a good sign at all. To make the answer meaningful, you need to see what a point of comparison is (for example, industrywide turnover statistics) so that you can see whether the organization is better or worse than the industry average.

"What is the average length of service?" and, *"What is the average age of your employees?"* are two variants that can say a lot about the organization you are considering and what your chances for advancement will be once you get there.

How long has this position existed in the organization? Has it changed recently?

How many people are you interviewing for this position?

Why are you seeking external candidates instead of promoting from within?

How many people have you interviewed so far?

How many more do you plan to interview?

When do you need to fill the position?

When will you make a hiring decision?

Who will make the hiring decision?

How much freedom would I have in determining my objectives and deadlines?

How much travel/overtime is usually expected?

How would my performance be measured?

How is successful performance rewarded?

How often would performance be measured?

Outside of my department, whom else would I work with?

What are some of the most difficult challenges I would face in this position?

What are your immediate goals and priorities for this position?

What did you like most about the person who last held this position?

What do people seem to like most/least about working here?

What do you see as my strengths/weaknesses for this position?

What is the average length of time employees stay in this position?

What projects or challenges could I expect to face if I am hired?

What support does this position get in terms of finances and people?

What would you like to see the person who fills this position do differently?

Where does this position typically lead?

Whom would I report to?

What is his or her background?

Who would I supervise and what are their backgrounds?

How do you see me fitting into the department/organization?

If you make me a job offer, how soon would you like me to start?

Is there anything I need to know about the organization or the job that has not yet been discussed?

Does the organization have a mission statement? May I read it?

The last question is a good one because it shows your awareness of a basic document that is commonly a part of most organizations' culture today. (Note that if the mission statement is on the organization's Website, you should have seen it.) The interviewer will appreciate the fact that you are interested, and the question may get the interviewer to share some insights tied to the organization's mission.

If you do ask questions about specific subjects, consider likely follow-up questions such as: *"Why are you interested in our foreign sales markets?"*

> *Even though the operations department has no direct link to foreign sales, I have been following stories about supply shortages and was curious if that was going to change the selling terms, affecting inventory turnover.*

Another follow-up question might be, "Your résumé does not show that you have any experience in that area; why are you asking?"

> *You are correct that I have not worked in a bank's retail sector, but I have always found that the front lines have a lot of impact on a bank's reputation and overall morale. Long teller lines and heavy staff turnover can generate negative reactions throughout the community and affect new business efforts.*

Be careful of the questions you ask so that you won't have to experience comebacks such as, "That was the lead story in yesterday's *Wall Street Journal*. Don't you read the business papers?" "Oh, I am glad that you brought up the subject of salary. What are you looking for?" "I thought the one thing you would really be interested in discussing would be _____, yet it was never mentioned."

15
Following Up After the Interviews

Two things are necessary after each interview: a debriefing and a thank-you. You should record your notes as soon as possible after each interview, while the material is fresh in your mind. Why is this important? If you are called back for another interview, you can call to mind what you liked and did not like about the organization or the job as well as your reactions to the entire experience. It is surprising that, after several interviews, the details and the interviewers may all tend to blur together. Additionally, it is another step in the learning process to give yourself credit for those interviews well done as well as note those areas that need improvement or responses that could have been more to the point.

This is also an opportunity to update your information file on the organization; what details or information did you obtain through the interview? Even if this particular job was not meant to be, you do not want to close any doors for yourself. Other job openings may come up at the same employer! How was the interviewer? (Refer to those points in Portrait of an Ideal Interviewer form from Chapter 1.) How would your rate your interviewer?

A Very Simple Thing— Thank You

After the interview an opportunity presents itself that many interviewees ignore. It is both good business sense and good manners to thank people for their time and effort. From a purely marketing point of view, it gives you one more chance to sell yourself and demonstrate that you were listening during the interview and that you do possess the rudiments of good manners.

Postinterview Debriefing

Date of interview: _____

Organization: _____

Interviewer: Name_____

      Title/department _____

Job opening:_____

      Job details: _____

_____

Your comments: _____

      Interviewer: _____

      Personal chemistry: _____

      Interview location: _____

Did you cover your agenda? _____

High points: _____

Could have done better: _____

Is there a substantive match? _____

Assess your chances: _____

Next step(s): _____

Unless your handwriting is totally illegible, a short, handwritten note is the essential follow-up to each interview. These notes should be in the mail to each interviewer within 24 hours of the meeting. As with all your other written communication, proofread for spelling and grammatical errors.

What should be in the thank-you note? A brief statement of appreciation for the time and effort taken to give you the chance to learn more about the organization and the job opening. Mention something specific from the interview.

The next paragraph should be a minisales pitch stating (again) why you are ideal for the job and that you do want it. It is surprising how many applicants do not ask for the job! Close with a statement of the next step, as you understand it, or what action you will take next.

Unless you are on a very informal, casual basis with the interviewer, send a hard-copy thank-you by mail—not an E-mail. If you have a reasonable belief that a decision will be made very soon, possibly before your thank-you letter is received, either drop off the thank-you in person or express your appreciation by telephone.

Thank-You Letter
Your letterhead or note paper, printed or handwritten

December 12, 2000

Ms. Evelyn Buckley
Public Relations Manager
ABC Company
123 Main Street
Anywhere, USA 12345

Dear Ms. Buckley:

It was a pleasure to meet with you and learn about ABC Company and its current goals. I have revisited ABC's Website and have seen the changes that you outlined to me; it is now a much more attractive and informative site. Of particular interest were the links to different departments.

After our discussion I feel that my qualifications and interests are ideal for the position of copywriter. My love of gardening and the outdoors should be a great match for a nursery and the work I had done at the Audubon Organization is related specifically to the types of news releases and copy that ABC needs. I feel that I could make a quick and substantial contribution at ABC.

You mentioned that a decision would be made within the next two weeks; if additional information or interviews are needed, I am available. I really am looking forward to hearing from you.

Sincerely,

J. J. Applicant

Was the interview a referral? Did someone pass on a lead to you that led to the interview? Do not forget to thank those who were instrumental in helping you get the interview. Telephone or write to thank them for their efforts, and bring them up to date on how you are doing with the hiring process. They may have suggestions or further leads for you.

Thank-You Letter for the Referral
Your letterhead or note paper, printed or handwritten

December 12, 2000

Ms. Sally Evans
123 Main Street
Anywhere, USA 12345

Dear Sally,

Yesterday I had the interview with Mr. _____. and he was as personable and informative as you had promised.

Unfortunately, the position of _____. had already been filled but he was suitably impressed with my résumé. The company is planning to open another office in the next 6 months and would be delighted to consider me for a position if I am interested. I certainly am!

It was a fortunate day for me when I met you at the sales seminar in Des Moines, and I thank you for your recommendation to _____.

I hope to see you before the next convention.

Sincerely yours,

J. J. Applicant

The "Fatal Attraction" Applicant

Do not become a stalker. There is enthusiasm in wanting to work for a particular organization and then there is being relentless. For many reasons, some individuals desire to work for a particular company in any capacity—*any job* will do, just so long as they can work there. These are fans, not employees, because they are too involved in the organization before they are even hired. High-profile, popular organizations may inspire such devotion, but do they really want such an employee? Companies in the entertainment or sports businesses (such as MTV, the NFL, Lifetime TV, or the WWF) attract a lot of fans that would *"just love to work there."* They send their untargeted résumés repeatedly to various individuals and seem to have a direct line on any new hire that may not have heard of them yet. If they do get an interview, afterward they will just be more relentless in their pursuit of a position at their dream company.

This is not the same as having a well-founded admiration for a particular organization and its product or culture. Curb your enthusiasm and still look to target specific jobs whose qualifications you match. Do not get into the *"I will take any job"* mantra during your interview; even if it is true, keep it to yourself. Also, sending different versions of your résumé geared to different job openings will not endear you to the company. Rather than showing you to be dedicated to getting a job there, you just come across as unfocused and unable to understand a simple no.

The same is true for sending gifts, making serial telephone calls, or sending multiple faxes; keeping your name in the interviewer's mind is quite different from making him or her look behind every pillar when going to the parking lot at the end of the workday.

Questions

If you have unresolved issues or wish to test your candidacy, contacting the interviewer is a proactive option.

> *When we met, you discussed an opening possibly becoming available in the IT (information technology) area. I have thought about it since, and I would like to learn more about it and see what I need to do to be considered for the position. I will call you on _____ to get additional details. Of course, if you prefer, please call.*
>
> *During our meeting, you discussed the importance of temperament in your strong-culture organization. Do I have the temperament to be successful there?*

During our meeting, we discussed your past successful and not-so-successful hires. We then moved on to other issues; please let me know what your projection for me is and what I need to do to get to the next step.

After meeting with you, I want more than ever to be part of your organization. Please let me know what school classes I should pursue as an appropriate course of study in preparation for applying for a job with you after graduation.

What is the next step?

When do you plan to check my references?

Who else will I have to meet with?

And the interviewer may have follow-up questions for you, too.

15.1 *May we have a list of references? May we contact your references?*

You may have a list that excludes my current employer. Let me call them first to let them know you will be calling.

15.2 *Thank you for sending over your portfolio/tape/disk. Explain to me how you came up with the idea for* _____*.*

They have grabbed the bait—show substance and your creativity. Don't say, "*Oh, I just tossed that off one morning.*" They want a show-and-tell, and this is the tell part.

15.3 *We are sorry, but we have made another selection for that position. You were a very strong candidate, however. Would you consider a related position in a different department?*

In meeting with you, I really came to appreciate the mission of XYZ Inc. and I would have preferred to have been accepted for the job I interviewed for, but am certainly willing to explore alternative positions. You are familiar with my skills and background; if you feel this other job is related to what I do, I would like to hear more.

15.4 *As promised, I am calling to let you know that we offered the position to another candidate, but you were our second choice.*

Has the other candidate accepted your offer? If not, would you then extend the offer to me? When is a decision expected?

Then follow-up.

When we spoke last on (date), you indicated that you expected a response on your job offer for _____ (position). Has the other candidate accepted?

Thanks for keeping me informed. If other similar positions open, I would like to be considered.

15.5   *I am sorry. After careful review of your qualifications, we have determined that you do not meet our needs at this time.*

That is disappointing because I really felt we hit it off in the interview, and I was certainly excited about the great opportunity. Can you share with me why I was not chosen?

Or

Can you make any suggestions as to how I can improve my presentation?

15.6   *We are very close to making a decision. Can you come in for another interview today?*

I am so interested in this position that even though I have other appointments, I will gladly come in. What time would you like me and whom will I be meeting with?

Surprise! You thought this organization was not interested. Grab your notes and do a quick review—if you really want this position. If you are not certain, you can buy some time by trying:

Could I call you back in about 15 minutes? I have an appointment this afternoon, and I am not certain I can reach this person to cancel. Thanks.

Now, aren't you glad you kept an interview log? Review your notes about the company and the interview itself; what you liked and what you did not like. If there is any doubt in your mind, take the interview unless it is at the expense of another interview that seems more promising.

16

Offers and Negotiations

Negotiation is a big part of the interview process. The worst thing to do is stop your interview preparations just when you are sure you will get an offer or immediately afterwards. Assuming that it is all over and that you can finally let your guard down can have you see the offer disappear. Your lack of interest and preparation at this point might lead to terms that are less than what you should have gotten. So if you have an offer in hand or feel one is imminent, reread your Needs versus Wants from Chapter 7. Have you changed any of the options you had selected? Have you learned a lot about reality and what is happening in the job market? Reconsider these points and be prepared to compare them to the actual job offer.

In most states, you can be fired at will—that is, at the will of the employer. You have been offered a job, but your employer has the right to rescind that offer at will as well. That is, if she or he has a change of heart (or mind), you no longer have an offer. What can change the circumstances to cause this traumatic event? Poor references on your part or a major change at the hiring organization (losing an expensive lawsuit or being acquired or sold).

Story #1. Recently, a marketing firm met with and offered an impressive applicant a job in business development for its online team. The hiring manager asked human resources if she could make the offer and said that she wanted to do it in person. The HR recruiter was impressed that as busy as the manager was, she wanted to take the time for a face-to-face meeting to make the offer. The meeting started well, but when the manager mentioned the salary, the candidate was visibly concerned. He said that he had two other *"compelling"* offers with higher compensation packages. The manager wanted to be sure that he really wanted the job with her organization in light of these two other compelling situations.

She mentioned that she would not engage in a bidding war but that she needed to know from the candidate that he really preferred her organization to the others. And if this was the case, then she would see whether something could be done about the salary she was offering. The candidate became inflexible and insisted that the amount be raised before he indicated his preference because he felt stating a preference would damage his negotiating position. He didn't believe that this impasse would lead to a withdrawal of a job offer. From the hiring manager's viewpoint, she was relieved that this disagreement surfaced so early because one of the major requirements of the position was the ability to make deals with others.

Story #2. An administrative assistant returned for a third interview to meet with a few more people because the hiring manager was going to make the offer in person and decided to do it after the third visit. During the visit, the candidate mentioned to one of the members of what would be her new team that she was looking forward to this job so that she could finally leave behind the duties of administrative assistant. (This was the title and responsibilities of the job she was being offered, and she had been through at least five interviews discussing that this would be the case!) Needless to say, the job was never offered.

The "New" Negotiations

Consider the entire interviewing process as one big negotiation. After each interview, the goal is to get to the next interview and so on through the process until you are finally offered the job. Those negotiations are all old once the offer is about to be made. You dealt with and handled that whole process successfully. Now it is time to deal with this new situation.

The negotiation process should be an opportunity for you to get the right package for *you*. If you don't, it is a lost opportunity.

Know Your Role

You need to remove your job applicant hat. You have been offered the job—orally or in writing—so now you are the candidate of choice but not yet the new hire. You need to show your professional maturity and ability, regardless of the job you are applying for, in closing the arrangement. Use this opportunity to show how astute you are and let the organization see how smart it was to hire you—never an easy task, so tread carefully.

Rules of Negotiation

❏ Be prepared. Research the job market, the organization, and management.

❏ Know what you want *and* what you need and the difference between the two.

❏ Understand your employer's needs.

❏ One size does *not* fit all. Each situation is different.

❏ Your image is on the line:

❏ Be professional. Be courteous. Be ethical. Be honest.

❏ It is not a contest. Do not look to score points.

❏ This is the first of many negotiations you will have with this employer if you accept the job. You will have future dealings; set the tone for your professional relationship.

❏ Do not burn your bridges. You never know when paths will cross again; be graceful in your dealings, even when you cannot accept the offer.

❏ Be creative. Consider trade-offs and compromises. Look at the entire offer, not just individual points.

❏ Know when to end the negotiation. Do not try for one more concession. If you have gotten what you have asked for, accept the offer. Also, know when there will be no more concessions and the offer must be declined, with your appreciation for being considered.

❏ Be gracious. No matter how the deal is finally struck, you are very happy to be joining their organization or happy to have met and dealt with the people involved.

Be Prepared

Before you meet with the people you will be negotiating with, get as much information as possible so that you can consider the details one by one as a package. Otherwise, you may try going back more than once and end up looking silly or worse—being bothersome—in their eyes. As you proceed through the interview process, continue doing research and check out news stories and information about the organization and the industry. (Refer to Super Sources and online resources cited in Chapter 7.)

When you are invited to one more meeting by your principal contact, ask about the purpose and agenda of the meeting and the name(s) and title(s) of the person(s) with whom you are being asked to meet, if you haven't met him, her, or them before. The person you are dealing with may or may not be astute and share the barest of information or may blurt out, *"We want to make you an offer in person."* It is more likely that the person will share some information. Take notes and listen carefully. If someone says something like, *"How quickly can you start?"* it is a solid sign he or she is eager to bring you on board and wants very much to close the deal. In response to, "When can we meet," be careful to not say, "Anytime, because I am doing nothing right now," unless this is really what you want your new employer to hear.

Be Considerate

When you are asked to be prepared, this includes knowing the person you are dealing with and the organization's environment. For starters, is it publicly traded or do you know if an IPO is planned? If so, are options a part of the offer? Before you ask about options, what have you learned about the company's practices concerning options—who gets them? How is the option price determined? What is the status of their options? Are the options below water at the time of the offer? Is the business growing or declining? The answers should have an effect on what questions you ask when you try to get yourself the best possible deal.

Be Decisive

When you get the offer, know what to do with it. Even if you had been tipped off, look excited. Remember, one reason the person making the offer wants to do so in person is to catch your immediate reaction. If you do not seem pleased, he or she will try to find out the reason(s).

Do not accept the offer immediately, unless that is your chosen strategy. We recommend that you ask to consider the offer overnight and give an answer the next day. If you are close to the weekend (it's Thursday), perhaps ask for the weekend to think about it. Under no circumstance take longer unless there is a good reason to and let the organization know what it is. If you are waiting for another offer, say so and ask for more time than you think it will take for you to get the other offer. If, for instance, your other offer is expected on Monday, assume you won't get it until the following Friday and say so. *"I must be honest with you. As you might expect, I have been interviewing with other companies, and I expect one to make me an offer this Friday. I really am excited at the prospects of working here, at _____, but I must be fair to myself and see what the other offer is."*

Negotiation Worksheet		
Use this to compare job offers or negotiation terms.		
Terms	**Job Offer**_____	**Job Offer**_____
Hire date		
Starting date		
Signing bonus		
Base salary		
Review date		
Profit sharing (%)		
Relocation expenses		
Interim accommodations		
Mortgage assistance		
Bridge loan		
Incentive bonus		
Options/equity		
Vacation time		
Car/transportation allowance		

Under no circumstances say that you will make a decision after discussing it with your spouse or significant other—even if this is true, don't say so. This is your offer—you need to make the decision. If you want to discuss it with someone else, that is your business.

Be Professional

Be gracious when the offer is extended, and, if you feel it is a generous offer, say so. If you don't think it is, and you are tempted to offer an alternative, be ready to mention the alternative amount or else wait for the rest of the offer to sink in (and an opportunity to discuss it with whomever).

If you have no intention of taking the offer, be careful because you need to consider whether the offer made will be the only one or whether it is open to negotiation. Are you just interested in seeing what you can get and you really don't want this job? You need to be prepared to determine whether anything offered will change your mind. If nothing will make you want the job, then do not under any circumstances start to negotiate.

If the job offer has real possibilities (*"If only it was not . . .* or *If only the job was . . ."*), then you have to expand your considerations beyond those typically stated in a job offer. What would make the job more attractive? Different reporting requirements? Your ability to bring on members of your own staff? A corner office? If you really do not want the job as stated in the job description but are willing to reconsider if there were some changes, then you might as well inquire. You are in a win-win situation because the worst that could happen is that the negotiations do not agree to any modifications and you don't accept the offer as is. Because you don't really want the job, you could be a hard negotiator, taking a stand and not wavering. Caution: if the points you raise are all accepted, you must accept the position. To not do so is unethical. Being professional means being ethical and not just spinning your wheels at the negotiating table.

Terms of the Job Offer

The *hire date* is the date you are offered the job. Compare this with the *start* or *employment date*, the date that you actually show up for work and commence employment. The employment date is the important one since it determines when you become eligible for benefits. Even if there is lag time between your start date and the date for the commencement of your benefits, the date used to trigger coverage is your start date if the benefits fall under ERISA (the Employment Retirement Income Security Act of 1974, as amended). This date may not be arbitrarily altered.

In a tight job market where available great workers are in short supply, a *signing* or *sign-on bonus* is frequently offered to workers throughout the ranks. The term "signing bonus" comes from professional sports. When the coveted player agrees to sign the contract, he or she is awarded a cash payment. For the rest of us, there usually is no contract, and if the employer you are joining has the right to release you at will, then you have the right to release yourself at will from the employer. With that in mind, private sector employers give a bonus to new hires but frequently delay payment until the person arrives for work. Also, the new employee may be asked to sign a statement saying that if she or he resigns before a certain date (6 months or a year), the employer has the right to take this bonus back in part if not in whole. The advantage to the employer is that the base salary offered is not affected; increases and profit sharing may be related only to the base salary. This may be a maneuver to reflect current market salaries without having to give pay increases to the current staff to bring them into line with a new hire.

If you are moving because of your new employer, you may want to ask for reimbursement or *relocation expenses* or, the best alternative, to have the employer handle the move for you. Some companies will even provide interim housing until you are able to purchase or rent in the area. If you need to purchase a residence, ask if the organization has a relationship with a bank that can provide a favorable mortgage or a bridge loan? One organization even provided boarding for a new executive's pet cats until the family's house was available.

Options—Funny Money?

Not too long ago, dot.coms had such cachet that vendors, suppliers, and employees were asked by the cash-strapped company to take payments in options. Then the truth came out. The number of options issued made their value negligible and the lack of earnings had eroded market price per share, bringing the option price over the market price. Employees frequently were the recipients of worthless options. The goal now is to take the cash and the options, too. If you can get both and stay at a competitive salary level (or even slightly higher), do so.

There are two types of option offers: pre-IPO and post-IPO. In pre-IPOs any stocks or options offered are privately held and therefore not under the scrutiny of the Securities Exchange Commission (SEC). In this type of situation, if options are offered, they can be set at any price that the organization (and its board and its venture capitalists) deems appropriate (a penny or a dollar a share for instance). When the company goes public, the gain is the difference in price between the cost of the option and the sale price. Once the company announces its intentions to go public, options may still be awarded but at the opening price of the stock to the public. It cannot be arbitrarily determined. The same is true after the company has gone public. Any options awarded then fall under the watchful eyes of the SEC.

Rescue Operations

In trying to keep their valued employees, if they feel an employee is looking to take another job, organizations are taking steps to head off resignations even before offers are made to job candidates. Some go so far as to assign a staff member with the sole task of surfing the Internet looking for employees who may be looking for positions, posting their résumés, or are even answering their own organization's blind online ad. Faster than they can download the résumé, the employer has the surprised employee in the office asking *"Are you happy here?"* and *"Why are you looking for another job?"*

Is your current employer actively trying to keep employees? Are perks such as foosball game machines, gym facilities, and espresso machines appearing? Have you heard stories of counteroffers being made to others? Look around and see what actions the employer and the human resources department take when they learn an employee is leaving. Do they pretend that it doesn't matter or that the organization loses only mediocre people? (*"They weren't all that good anyway."*) There is a prevailing myth, probably perpetuated by remaining staff and management, that the best choose to stay rather than the other way around.

Or does the organization immediately meet with the employee to determine if anything can be done to persuade the departing employee to stay? Quite frankly, if your current employer could care less about whether you stay or go, that is one more reason to consider leaving.

Why Did You Start Looking for Another Job?

Before you accept another offer and before you resign, reexamine your reasons for starting your job search.

1. What is wrong with your current situation?

   _____

2. What will you expect from a new job?

   _____

3. What do you think you can actually get from your next job?

   _____

4. What kind of work environment works best for you?

   _____

5. What skills do you want to use?

   _____

6. What don't you want to do?

   _____

Resigned to Leaving?

Before submitting your resignation, review one more time your reasons for deciding that the unknown outside opportunity is something you prefer over your current situation. Remind yourself of the reasons you decided to go through the major task of looking for another job when your time could have been used for other, more enjoyable pursuits. If you believe the "handwriting is on the wall," do you feel you might be offered a "package" (severance and benefits) to resign? You need not be a senior executive to be offered a package.

If you are intent on resigning, you must be sure that you have a bona fide offer. The interviewer saying that he or she is *"really impressed,"* that you are *"the best candidate we have seen,"* and that *"you would really be an asset to our organization"* are *not* job offers. A job offer can be a spoken offer extended to you, but the preferred offer is in writing. A written job offer should contain the same terms quoted to you orally. These basic terms include:

Job title

Starting compensation including salary, bonuses, incentives, any other payments, and benefit package

Starting date and details of reporting to work

E-mail Job Offer

Subj: Publicist Job Opening

Date: 11/23/00 10:09 A.M. Pacific Daylight Time

From: ImaRecruiter@job4u.com(I.M. Recruiter)

To: N. V. Adams

Dear N _____,

It was our last interview yesterday, and we are delighted to offer the position of publicist in our Los Angeles office to you. The station manager would like to make the offer to you personally, according to the terms we have discussed, on Thursday at our headquarters at 11:30 A.M. We would like you to join us for lunch afterwards.

We are all looking forward to your joining us next month.

Regards,

Ima

When given an oral offer, take notes and wait to compare it to the actual paperwork. Often an oral offer will open the door to negotiations, which are culminated in the written offer. An E-mail offer may take the place of an oral offer but not a written offer.

Offer Letter

Organization letterhead

April 5, 2001

Mrs. Nola Evans
123 Main Street
Anywhere, USA 12345

Dear Mrs. Evans,

On behalf of _____ Corporation, I am delighted to offer you the position of office manager at our headquarters, as we had discussed in your interview on March 10.

We would like your starting date to be April 18, 2001, at an annual salary of $105,000. Your first salary review date would be in 12 months, at which time you would be eligible for a salary increase. Executive salaries are paid semimonthly, on the 1st and 15th of every month. You are eligible for all employee benefits as of your starting date; such benefits are subject to change.

All our employees are subject to a 3-month introductory period; yours will end on July 18, 2001. _____ Corporation has the right to terminate your employment at any time during or after the introductory period. At the end of the introductory period, your performance will be evaluated to determine if it has met the requirements for the position.

Please report to my office at 8:45 A.M. on April 16 to receive our employee orientation package and to complete some additional paperwork; on the 18th you will be expected to report to Ms. _____, Room _____ for a 2-hour orientation commencing at 10:00 A.M.

Please sign and return a copy of this letter as an acknowledgment that you have read and understood the terms of the offer.

We are looking forward to having you on our team.

Signed

(copy)   Acknowledged _____ date _____

Counteroffers

If an organization meets quickly with an employee who submits his or her resignation, there is a great likelihood that it is an organization that makes counteroffers. Usually counteroffers are about money. Other issues can be a factor, but more often than not the issue is money. For instance, a person may be leaving because she or he is tired of the tension buildup that comes from the one and one-half hours it takes to go thirty-five miles to and from her or his residence. It could be a new baby. It could be a spouse's transfer or acceptance of a job offer that requires relocation. An organization should commence salvage measures as soon as it learns an employee is considering a new employer, ideally before a job offer is made to him or her. The current employer does not know if the employee is truly serious about leaving the organization or is window-shopping.

Research studies suggest that employees who received counteroffers remain with the organization for just under 2 years after the offer is made and accepted. A lot of that has to do with the discomfort that both parties feel from the breakdown of trust. Employers wonder about the lack of loyalty, and the decision an employee makes to leave once certainly is an indication that it may happen again: *"Planning should be done now in the event that employee X decides to leave again. We don't ever want to be caught short again."*

Questions

You have more questions before you can close the deal.

When will your offer be sent to me?

You want the offer in writing for three reasons.

1. You want to be sure there is no misunderstanding; you are being offered the job you interviewed for according to the terms discussed and negotiated.
2. It is an opportunity to see how effective the organization is with something as important as offer letters.
3. This is a sneaky way to gain time to consider the offer.

Another way to ask the question is, *"May I have this offer in writing?"* But stated this way, this simple request may be a dangerous one. For starters, what if the person you are speaking to says *"No, because we don't put our offers in writing."* Additionally the person making the offer may take this as an indication that you don't trust him or her.

Is the salary negotiable?

Are there opportunities for bonuses or any other form of incentive?

When will I be reviewed? Is there an opportunity for a salary review at the same time?

Is there a signing bonus?

Frankly, the only thing preventing me from accepting is my desire to maintain a working relationship with my executive assistant, who has been superb. Is there a possibility that I could bring him on board when I start, since I will have to hire staff?

May I have a copy of my benefits in writing?

You should get the plan booklets as well as any other printed material the employer gives its new employees. The reason for taking the actual documents that describe the various plans is that these documents provide the details and terms of what is covered, and this information is not being filtered through the eyes of others (who may in fact be wrong).

Asking for the benefits in writing also gives you an opportunity to find answers to any questions that you have a special interest in without seeming overly concerned about this area. You may be concerned about coverage for a specific illness, for instance, but asking may lead to other questions. By seeing what you have in writing, you are not indicating what is of particular interest. In addition, by asking for the material, you are demonstrating your sophistication in this area as well as getting a more accurate picture of what the employer does for its employees.

"When do you need my answer?" Or *"Thank you very much. It is an attractive offer. Let me review it and consider it briefly. I will let you know my decision on _____, if that meets with your approval."* These are two versions of the same question. But notice that in the first approach, the employer gets to set the time; in the second, you do.

I am planning to get married in September (during the first year of my employment). Included in those arrangements is a ___ day trip to Bora Bora; will I be able to have the time off?

If you have planned this vacation, now is the time to ask. Earlier would have been a mistake as would be later (hiding bad news). By doing it now, it becomes one more negotiating point. Don't suggest you take it without pay. Let them ask if you would be willing to—just remember they may not!

17
Epilogue

If we do not spend 4 hours on placing a man and placing him right,
we'd spend 400 hours cleaning up after our mistakes.

—Alfred Sloan, creator of General Motors

Even though it is not politically correct to say "man" nowadays and it
may take much more than 4 hours to hire and more than 400 hours to correct a hiring mistake, the sentiment stands correct.

Doing it right the first time is still the best option for both the candidate
and the hiring organization. No one wants to end a job search in a job that
just "does not work out."

Employees from many generations work together and share different
values, work ethics, and expectations. Managers are expected to deal with
them all, as well as compete globally and deal with technological revolu-
tions. Change is omnipresent and is occurring at a furious pace. Knowledge and the ability to learn and adapt are at a premium—on both sides
of the interviewing desk.

It has been years since the concept of job security has been thought of
as anything more than an oxymoron. Estimates place the number of new
businesses started daily at over 3,000, while over 2,500 fail each day; that
is a lot of employee displacement! Nearly 2,000 businesses change their
addresses daily!

Eight change their names each day. Change is the norm. Businesses in
both the real and cyber world start and close with lightning speed. Mom
and Pop drugstores are being replaced by chain stores. Who is doing business is changing as fast as how the business is done.

Yet job interviews remain constant. The face-to-face assessment and inquiry continue to be the best ways to judge who works where. Technology has entered the picture, but it is still human judgment that holds the
power to extend that sought after job offer.

The other constant, at least for the near term in this dynamic market, is that everyone is always looking for another job. People are looking actively, just "poking around," or keeping an eye out for a better opportunity.

Because the stakes are so high and the costs associated with making a bad hiring decision—for both the candidate and the employer—the interview remains the essential linchpin in the decision of who gets hired and at what price.

Give attention to your interview preparation. You will be glad you did.

Index